Food in a minute...
the cookbook

> The Heinz Wattie's products used in filming the programmes that make *Food in a Minute*™ were correct at the time of filming. However, from time to time names and can sizes alter, or products may be deleted. Please use a similar product if this should happen — **Allyson Gofton**

Tableware and props kindly supplied by:

ALLIUM INTERIORS, Kingdon Street, Newmarket, Auckland; **CORSO DE' FIORI**, George Street, Parnell, Auckland; **COUNTRY ROAD**, Broadway, Newmarket, Auckland; **FREEDOM FURNITURE**, Broadway, Newmarket, Auckland; **LIVING AND GIVING**, Broadway, Newmarket, Auckland; **MILLY'S KITCHEN SHOP**, Ponsonby Road, Ponsonby, Auckland; **NEST**, Broadway, Newmarket, Auckland; **STUDIO OF TABLEWARE**, Mount Eden Road, Mount Eden, Auckland; **TRUMPS**, Remuera Road, Newmarket, Auckland.

ISBN 1-86958-895-9

Original text, recipes and photographs created by Allyson Gofton for Heinz Wattie's Limited

© 2001 Recipes and photographs — Heinz Wattie's Limited

© 2001 Food in a Minute™ — Heinz Wattie's Limited

© 2001 Design and format — Hodder Moa Beckett Publishers Limited

Published in 2001 by Hodder Moa Beckett Publishers Limited
[a member of the Hodder Headline Group],
4 Whetu Place, Mairangi Bay, Auckland, New Zealand

Reprinted 2002

Designed and produced by Hodder Moa Beckett Publishers Limited
Photography by Alan Gillard and Nick Tressider
Colour separations by Microdot, Auckland
Printed by Toppan Printing Company, Hong Kong

Food in a Minute, Watties, The Good Taste Company device, Hellaby's, Bit on the Side and Greenseas are trademarks of Heinz Wattie's Limited and its associated entities and are used under licence.

All rights reserved. No part of this publication may be reproduced or transmitted in any form or by any means, electronic or mechanical, including photocopying, recording, or any information storage and retrieval system, without permission in writing from the publisher.

Food in a minute...
the cookbook

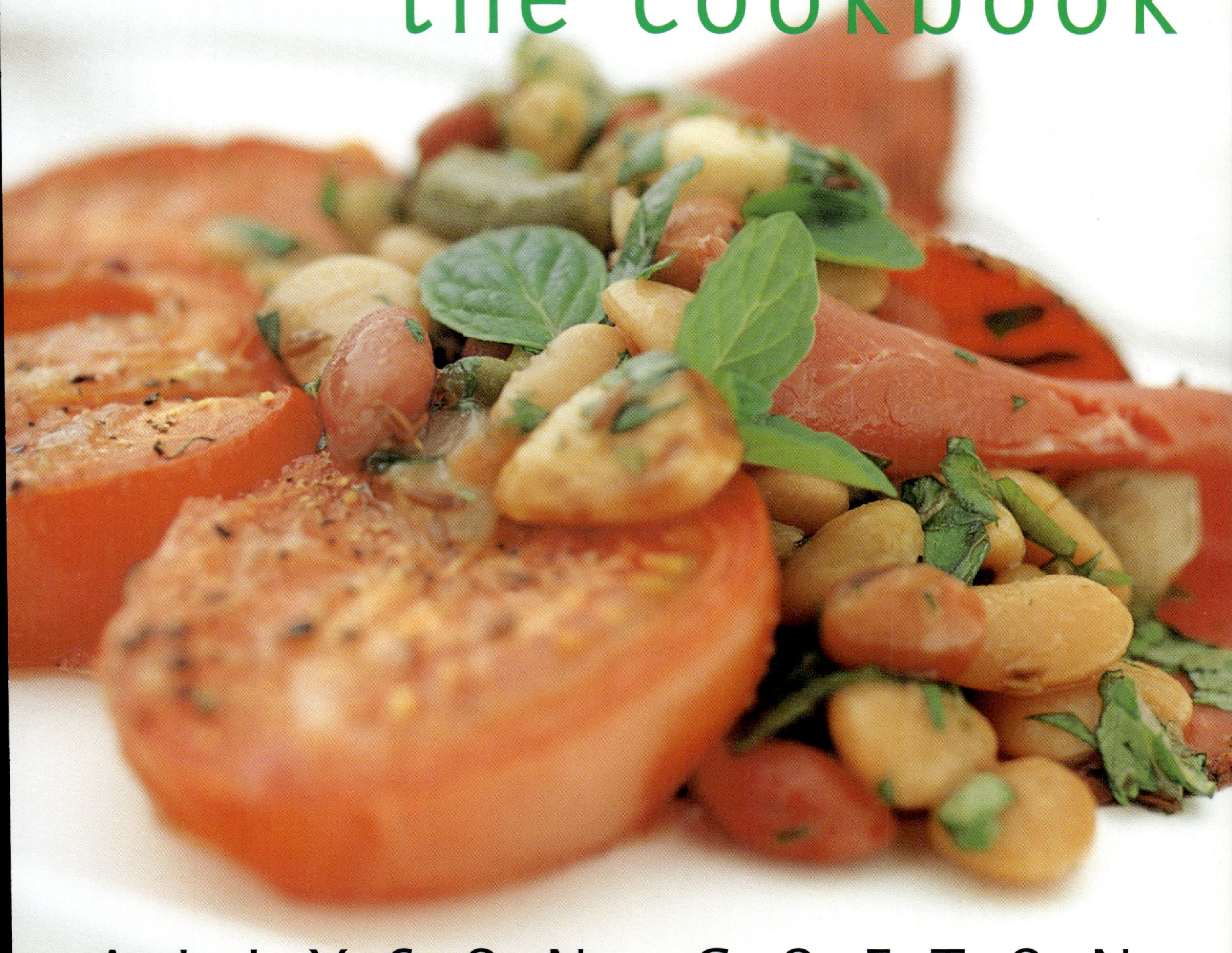

ALLYSON GOFTON

{contents}

introduction
7

soups and nibbles
9

eggs and cheese
21

salads and light meals
33

pasta and rice
53

chicken and turkey
71

beef and lamb
91

pork and ham
123

tuna and other fish
135

vegetarian
145

baking and desserts
155

index
175

{introduction}

This book celebrates five successful years of *Food in a Minute*™. What began as an idea created and formatted by communication whizz Mike O'Sullivan has since its inception been sponsored by Wattie's, nurtured by me and creatively filmed by the team at Tiger Films and Channel i. The programme has now become a regular part of our daily lives. Our home-grown idea instantly became a smash hit and remains so after five years and 250 programmes. The Wattie's *Food in a Minute*™ programme has, under Mike's guidance, recently spread its wings across the Tasman. We've gone international and are doing well.

The *Food in a Minute*™ cookbooks have shared this success, with more than 250,000 copies sold during the last five years. *Food in a Minute*™: *The Cookbook* is a collection of new food ideas combined with your favourite recipes. When I began to gather together the recipes for this book it was an opportunity to look over those ideas that were great winners and to let you know of some that were not so popular. It was also a chance to think about what our *Food in a Minute*™ team had learned.

Tuscan Chicken was our very first recipe, the one we used on our trial programme that persuaded Wattie's to sponsor the *Food in a Minute*™ idea. Tuscan Chicken encompassed then, much as it does now, what we wanted *Food in a Minute*™ to be — food ideas that are easy to prepare and cook, a type of 'healthy food assembly'. After all, who has hours to cook each evening? The ideas were to be nutritious with a good balance of all foods, allowing for a little indulgence here and there *and* the magic ingredient — a little Wattie's to make the flavour great and life easier.

Tuscan Chicken was followed by French Beef and Mushroom Cottage Pie topped with the now famous Wattie's Pom Poms. This recipe more than any other indelibly engraved *Food in a Minute*™ on your hearts and our culture. Within one week of its showing we sold over three months' supply of Wattie's Pom Poms and created a Kiwi classic from the British cottage pie, only easier and tastier.

In one *Food in a Minute*™ programme last summer we combined smoked chicken with melons, tomatoes and pesto dressing, and were simply amazed at your response. This no-cook, great tasting, toss-together salad became an instant success, with smoked chickens and pesto dressing selling out in the shops. Callers to *Next* magazine for the recipe almost drove our publishing assistant Lynette Begovich crazy as viewers clamoured to get the recipe.

After another hit recipe in winter one year, we had an offer (only half-serious!) from a local butcher to start farming five-legged sheep. He could not meet demand after we showed a Kiwi favourite — lamb shanks in wine. Some favourites are always winners.

One learning experience was the recipe for Peanut Chocolate Chip Cookies prepared from peanut butter, sugar, egg and chocolate chips. Unfortunately we are classic bakers in New Zealand, and the concept of making biscuits without beating butter and sugar was too foreign. Yet again, we learned more about our culture in relation to food and that some shortcuts do not go down well.

tuscan chicken **page 78**

french beef and mushroom cottage pie **page 99**

lamb shanks **page 116**

no-fuss apple tart page 158

butter chicken page 79

So, as you can see, over the years at *Food in a Minute*™ we've become pretty knowledgeable about what you eat, when you eat and how you like to eat.

As the pages of this book started to come together, what also became apparent was how these days food and fashion go hand in hand. What we want is in-season family meals at home and international-style dishes — *and* we want it quickly. I am reminded as I travel the country demonstrating, that you, like me and our *Food in a Minute*™ team, are so short on time to cook that you want easy, healthy ideas that can be prepared with a minimum of fuss and skill, but still be 'up there' with food fashion.

Food in a Minute™ has kept up with the trends every year. Along with our more traditional family meals we have added Thai and other Asian-style dishes, shown how to cook with vermicelli noodles and orzo pasta, presented Italian-influenced foods such as Potato and Parmesan Cakes with Tuscan Sauce and focaccia bread-based snacks and introduced Indian Curries and even California Sushi Rolls to the repertoire.

It wasn't just the recipes in this book that had to keep up with the latest food trends — the pictures had to look great too. We all chuckled as we reviewed the dated looking photographs from the earliest books. So we re-photographed almost all the recipes to add new life to these great ideas. Favourite recipes, such as No Fuss Apple Tart, Quick Mussel Chowder, Smoked Chicken and Melon Salad, Butter Chicken and Rogan Josh are still as popular as ever. We just serve them differently — with a little less fuss and a lot more style. Crisp, clean, light and stylish, our *Food in a Minute*™ recipes, look more mouthwatering than ever.

Putting this book together was a huge task, and I owe my thanks to the team who propped, cooked, styled, typed, proofed and then cleaned and cleaned — food assistants, clever cooks and stylists Ann Boardman and Tracey Sunderland; personal assistant Mary-Lou McGarry; typist Tonita Burrage-Thorpe; and props person and inspiration guru Sarah-Jane Gillies. Behind the lenses Nick Tresidder and Alan Gillard gave us new photography style. Publisher Hodder Moa Beckett has created a fresh look and I am grateful to Linda Cassells for her infinite patience and Nick Turzynski for his creative new look.

Special thanks to Heinz Wattie's and Mike O'Sullivan for their continued support and encouragement, and to energetic and dedicated food economist Di Handley.

Wattie's and *Food in a Minute*™ want to inspire you with great food ideas — ones that are easy on the pocket, tasty but uncomplicated, and that encourage you to be creative in a kitchen. I hope that *Food in a Minute*™: *The Cookbook* will only enhance that.

Allyson Gofton

soups
and nibbles

{soups and nibbles}
tips and hints

1

1 Homemade stocks definitely taste better. They can be prepared from inexpensive ingredients and frozen in cup lots for practical use at a later date. Don't forget to label them so you know if they are beef or chicken.

2 When using Wattie's frozen vegetables, always seal any remaining vegetables securely to avoid freezer burn and nutrition loss.

2

3 When cooking with leeks, the easiest way to clean them is to cut them lengthwise into quarters and rinse under cold water. This way you will find any small dirt particles that may have been trapped in the leeks during growth.

4 To chop an onion quickly and easily, peel it leaving the core end intact. Cut in half through the core end. Slice thinly across the onion and then chop finely. The thickness of both slicing actions will determine the size of the dice.

3

4

5 Never put good knives in a dishwasher. The harsh action will 'pit' the fine edges of your knife. Always wash by hand.

6 Once you add milk to a chowder, remember not to boil it as this will cause the milk to curdle. The same can happen to coconut milk.

7 The easiest way to quickly grill red peppers is to cut them in quarters, discarding the core and seeds. Press the quarters flat and place on a foil-lined baking tray. Grill under a high heat until they are blistered and blackened. Cover with a piece of foil and allow to stand until cooked enough to peel. Do not peel under water as it washes away valuable flavour.

8 For easy measurements 1 cup of grated cheese equals 100 grams.

9 Always keep mushrooms in a paper bag; this will prevent them from sweating and they will keep longer.

10 Open your Wattie's asparagus spears upside down, so when you turn them into a sieve to drain you will not damage their tender tips.

smoked fish chowder

1 large onion, peeled and diced
2–3 stalks celery, trimmed and diced
2 potatoes, peeled and diced
50 grams butter
3 tblsp flour
2 tsp mild curry powder
2 cups fish or vegetable stock
2 cups milk
350 grams smoked fish, flaked
2 cups frozen **Wattie's Freshlock™ Mixed Vegetables**
1/4 cup cream (optional)
2–3 tblsp chopped fresh parsley or chives
salt and pepper to season

1. Cook the onion, celery and potatoes in the butter for 3–5 minutes until softened. Add the flour and curry powder and cook for 1–2 minutes.

2. Stir in the stock and milk and allow to simmer for 5 minutes. Add the smoked fish and mixed vegetables and allow to poach for around 5 minutes.

3. Stir in the cream, if using, and parsley or chives and season with salt and pepper. Serve in deep bowls.

Serves 4

quick mussel chowder

16–20 cooked mussels
dash of oil
2 stalks celery, trimmed and finely diced
1 carrot, peeled and finely diced
1/2 leek or 1 small onion, finely diced
1 tsp curry powder
2 x 535 gram cans **Wattie's Very Special Creamy Pumpkin Soup**
sour cream and chopped fresh parsley to garnish

1. Chop mussels roughly.

2. In a saucepan heat the dash of oil and gently cook the celery, carrot, leek or onion and curry powder for about 3–5 minutes until softened but not browned.

3. Stir in the 2 cans of soup and bring to a simmer. Reduce heat but do not boil. Add the mussels to the soup and warm through.

4. Ladle into warm soup bowls and garnish with a dollop of sour cream and chopped parsley.

Serves 4

chunky bacon and kumara chowder with orange and bacon scones

chunky bacon and kumara chowder

500–600 grams orange kumara, peeled and chopped*
2 onions, peeled and chopped
1 tsp minced garlic
1 tsp curry powder
3 cups chicken or vegetable stock
1 tblsp butter or oil
4–6 thick slices rindless bacon, diced
750 gram packet frozen **Wattie's Freshlock™ Chuckwagon Corn**
1/2 cup milk or cream (optional)
salt and pepper to season
chopped fresh parsley to garnish

orange and bacon scones

50 grams butter
2 cups self-raising flour, sifted
3/4 cup milk
4–6 rashers bacon, cooked until crispy
grated rind 2 oranges
1 cup grated edam, gouda or colby cheese
1 egg

*This is about 3 medium-sized kumara.

chunky bacon and kumara chowder

1. Place the kumara, onions, garlic, curry powder and stock in a large saucepan. Cover and boil for 15 minutes or until the kumara is tender. Transfer (carefully) to a food processor and process until smooth.

2. Heat the butter or oil in the saucepan, add the bacon and cook until crispy. Drain off any excess oil.

3. Return the kumara to the saucepan and add the corn and milk or cream if using. Reheat and season.

4. Serve garnished with parsley and accompanied by the Orange and Bacon Scones.

orange and bacon scones

1. Cut in the butter into the flour until the mixture resembles fine crumbs. Stir in the milk to make a soft dough.

2. Roll out on a floured board to 2 cm thickness. Cut into rounds and place on a greased tray. Mix the topping ingredients together and dot on top of the scones.

3. Bake at 230°C for 12–15 minutes until cooked.

Serves 6

top smoked fish chowder
middle right chunky bacon and kumara chowder
left quick mussel chowder
bottom right orange and bacon scones

minted pea soup with warm blue cheese toasts

minted pea soup
25 grams butter
1 onion, peeled and sliced
1 large potato, peeled and diced
5 cups chicken stock
750 gram packet frozen **Wattie's Freshlock™ Baby Peas**
½ cup cream
salt and pepper to season
2 tblsp chopped fresh mint (optional)

warm blue cheese toasts
1 ciabatta loaf or ½ French loaf, finely sliced
2 tblsp oil or melted butter
100 grams each blue cheese and cream cheese

minted pea soup
1. Heat the butter in a large saucepan and add the onion. Cook for 1–2 minutes, then add the potato and stock.
2. Bring to the boil and simmer for 5 minutes. Add the peas and simmer for a further 5–8 minutes until the peas are soft but not overcooked.
3. Place all the ingredients in a food processor and process well until smooth. Return to the saucepan and add the cream. Season with salt and pepper. Add the mint before serving with Warm Blue Cheese Toasts.

warm blue cheese toasts
1. Brush bread with oil or butter and place on a greased baking tray. Grill on one side until golden then turn over.
2. Mix the blue cheese and cream cheese together and spread onto the untoasted side. Grill until golden.

Serves 6

hummus

300 gram can **Craig's Chickpeas in Brine**, well drained
1–2 tsp minced garlic
½ tsp each salt and cayenne pepper
2 tblsp oil (olive is nice here)
juice 1 lemon

1. Put everything in the food processor and process until smooth.

Makes ¾ cup

roasted red pepper hummus
1 red pepper
1 basic Hummus recipe

1. Cut the red pepper into quarters, discarding the core and seeds. Grill under a high heat until well blackened. Cool and then peel away the charred skin.
2. Place the pepper and hummus in a food processor and process until smooth.

Makes 1 cup

chilli tuna and hummus dip
85 gram pouch **Greenseas Sweet Thai Chilli Tuna**
1 basic Hummus recipe
2 tblsp chopped fresh coriander
1 tblsp chopped fresh mint
1 tsp minced garlic
½ tsp minced ginger

1. Mix all ingredients together.

Makes 1 cup

chicken rarebit

2½ cups grated tasty cheddar cheese
25 grams butter
2–3 tblsp **Lea & Perrins Worcestershire Sauce**
¼ cup dark beer

salt and pepper to season
4 slices thick white bread (focaccia is good here)
1 cup leftover cold meat (chicken, ham or beef)

1. Put the cheese, butter, Worcestershire sauce and beer into a saucepan and stir over a low heat until the cheese has melted and the mixture is smooth and creamy. Season with salt and pepper.
2. Toast the bread under a grill on one side only and then top the ungrilled side with a little of the cold meat.
3. Spoon an equal amount of the cheese mixture over the top. Grill under a high heat until golden and the cheese is bubbling. Serve immediately.

Serves 2–4 (depending on appetite!)

grilled focaccia with tomato salsa

350 grams button mushrooms, very finely sliced
dash oil
300 gram jar **Wattie's Bit on the Side Tomato Tango Salsa**
½ cup grated parmesan or cheddar cheese or crumbled feta cheese
2 tblsp finely chopped oregano or use 2 tsp dried
1 large piece focaccia bread

1. Cook the mushrooms in the oil in a frying pan over a high heat until the mushrooms are well browned. Cool.
2. Mix the mushrooms with the salsa, cheese and oregano.
3. Spread the mixture evenly over the focaccia bread.
4. Fan grill at 200°C for 10 minutes until the top is hot and the bread warm. Serve in wedges as a nibble or alongside a barbecue.

Makes 1 or **Serves** 6

asparagus filo rolls

125 grams cream cheese
2 tblsp chopped fresh herbs (tarragon, parsley, chives, chervil)
1 tblsp wholeseed mustard
4 rashers bacon, cooked until crisp (optional)
about 12 sheets filo pastry
75 grams butter, melted
340 gram can **Wattie's Asparagus Spears**, well drained
2–3 tsp sesame seeds (optional)

1. Mix together the cream cheese, herbs, mustard and bacon if using.
2. Take 1 sheet of filo pastry and brush lightly with butter. Cut in half crosswise and then fold each half in half again. Spread each piece with a little of the cream cheese mixture in the centre and place 1 asparagus spear on top. Roll up to securely enclose the asparagus.
3. Place on a greased baking tray and brush with butter to glaze. Sprinkle with sesame seeds if wished. Repeat with the remaining ingredients.
4. Bake at 200°C for 14–15 minutes. Serve warm with drinks.

Makes 20 rolls

cheese dip with spicy wedges

1 tblsp oil
2 spring onions, minced or finely chopped
1–2 tsp minced garlic
2 tsp ground cumin
1 tsp ground coriander
1 tsp ground paprika
300 gram jar **Wattie's Bit on the Side Tomato Tango Salsa**
125 grams cream cheese
¼ cup cream
1½ cups grated tasty cheddar cheese
1 tblsp cornflour
pepper to season

to serve
700 gram packet **Wattie's Crisp N'Spicy Wedges**
crudités (vegetable sticks and baby tomatoes)

1. Heat the oil in a saucepan and cook the spring onion, garlic, cumin, coriander and paprika for 2–3 minutes until quite fragrant.
2. Add the tomato salsa to the saucepan with the cream cheese and stir until melted. Add the cream, grated cheese and cornflour. Allow to cook over a low heat, stirring all the time until thickened and hot. Season with pepper.
3. Place the spicy wedges on a baking tray and cook according to the directions on the back of the packet.
4. Serve the cheese dip in a large bowl with the spicy wedges and vegetables.

Serves 6 as nibbles

creamy lemon tuna dip

150 gram pouch **Greenseas Lemon and Cracked Pepper Tuna**
250 gram tub spreadable cream cheese
¼ cup unsweetened plain yoghurt
2 tblsp finely chopped parsley
grated rind and juice 1 lemon
strips of lemon rind

1. Mix together the tuna, cream cheese, yoghurt, parsley and lemon rind and juice. Serve on crackers garnished with lemon rind.

Makes 2 cups

potato kebabs with avocado dip

avocado dip
2 avocados, halved, stoned and peeled
1 tsp minced garlic
¼ cup Eta Avocado and Garlic Dressing
2 tblsp lemon juice
1 tsp ground cumin
1 tsp ground coriander
½ tsp ground chilli
2 tblsp chopped fresh parsley or coriander

potatoes
500 grams baby new potatoes, washed

avocado dip

1 Blend together the avocado, garlic, dressing, lemon juice, cumin, coriander, chilli and parsley or coriander in a food processor or blender until smooth.

2 Place in a serving bowl; cover and refrigerate.

3 Cook the potatoes in boiling, salted water for 10–15 minutes or until tender. Drain. Serve the potatoes on skewers with the Avocado Dip.

Makes 1½ cups

mini cheese muffins

2 cups self-raising flour
1 tsp salt
1 tblsp any mustard powder
1 tsp paprika
1 cup grated cheddar cheese
1 cup Eta Mayo Tangy American Style Mayonnaise
1 cup milk
½ cup extra grated cheese

1 Sift the flour, salt, mustard powder and paprika together into a bowl. Stir in the cheese and make a well in the centre.

2 Mix the mayonnaise and milk together and carefully stir into the dry ingredients. Three-quarters fill 36 well-greased mini muffin tins. Sprinkle with extra cheese on top.

3 Bake at 200°C for 12 minutes or until cooked. Serve as is or halve and fill with a slice of brie and reheat at 180°C for 5 minutes.

Makes 36

chinese chicken nibbles

500 grams Tegel Chicken Nibbles
1 tsp minced garlic
1 tsp minced ginger
1 tsp Chinese five spice powder (optional)
¼ cup **Wattie's Asian Sweet Soy Sauce**
2 tblsp **Wattie's Asian Oyster Sauce**
2 tblsp sherry

1. Place the chicken nibbles in a snaplock bag with the garlic, ginger, spice, soy sauce, oyster sauce and sherry. Seal the bag and toss to coat evenly. Refrigerate for 1 hour or up to 1 day.
2. Place the chicken on a foil-lined baking tray and bake at 200°C (fan-bake 180°C) for 15–18 minutes. Alternatively, pan-fry or barbecue.
3. Serve the chicken nibbles with the Cucumber Chilli Dipping Sauce or Yoghurt Chilli Dipping Sauce.

Makes about 20 nibbles

cucumber chilli dipping sauce

½ telegraph cucumber
¼ cup **Wattie's Asian Chilli Sauce**
¼ cup water
2 tblsp chopped fresh mint

1. Halve the cucumber and scoop out the seeds. Grate on a fine grater and then mix with the chilli sauce, water and mint.

Makes ¾ cup

yoghurt chilli dipping sauce

¼ cup non-fat, plain yoghurt
¼ cup **Wattie's Asian Chilli Sauce**
2 tblsp chopped fresh mint

1. Mix the yoghurt, chilli sauce and mint together.

Makes ½ cup

corn tarts and variations

12 slices sandwich-slice bread, crusts removed
50 grams butter, melted
410 gram can **Wattie's Cream Style Corn**
1 egg
½ cup grated cheese (optional)
2–3 tblsp cream (optional)

1 Brush the slices of bread liberally with butter on one side. Place the buttered side down in 12 muffin tins.

2 Bake at 180°C for 10–12 minutes until the bread cases are golden and crispy.

3 Mix together the corn, egg, cheese and cream if using.

4 Spoon equal amounts of the corn mixture into the bread cases.

5 Return to the oven for 15 minutes until well risen and golden.

Makes 12

olive and tomato tartlets

12 pre-cooked bread cases
400 gram can **Wattie's Italian Seasoned Tomatoes**
1 red pepper, finely chopped
100 grams diced or crumbled feta cheese
2 tblsp chopped olives
1–2 anchovies, finely chopped (optional)
½ tblsp finely chopped fresh basil or parsley

1 Mix together the tomatoes with the pepper, crumbled feta cheese, olives, anchovies (if using) and herbs.

2 Spoon into the 12 crispy bread cases. Bake at 180°C for 12–15 minutes until hot and golden.

Makes 12

creamy tuna tartlets

12 pre-cooked bread cases
180 gram can **Greenseas Tuna in Oil**, well drained
3 spring onions, finely chopped
1 tsp minced garlic
1 cup grated cheddar cheese
½–1 cup sour cream
¼ cup finely chopped fresh parsley or chervil
1 egg

1 Mix together the tuna, spring onion, garlic, cheddar cheese, sour cream, parsley or chervil and egg.

2 Spoon the mixture into 12 crispy bread cases. Bake at 180°C for 12–15 minutes until hot and golden.

Makes 12

eggs and cheese

{eggs and cheese} tips and hints

1

1 To boil perfect eggs, place them carefully in boiling water and bring quickly back to the boil. Stir occasionally to centre the egg yolk. Once boiling, cook:
- 3–4 minutes for soft
- 5–6 minutes for medium-cooked yolk
- 8–10 minutes for firm, hard-boiled yolk.

Times are taken for size 7 eggs at room temperature. For eggs straight from the refrigerator, add an extra minute's cooking time.

2 If you overcook an egg it has a grey rim around the outside of the yolk. It is perfectly all right to eat, but doesn't look great.

2

3 To easily peel a hard-boiled egg, once cooked crack the shell and plunge it into cold water. When cool enough to handle, peel. Peeled, hard-boiled eggs will become tough if exposed to the air for too long, so keep them refrigerated in a lidded container for up to 4–5 days.

4 The white of an egg is firm when fresh and becomes thinner as the egg ages. To know if your eggs are still fresh enough to eat, place them in a jug of water. They should sink or stay near the bottom. If they float or sit towards the top, the eggs are stale and should be discarded.

3

4

5 Eggs will whip better and will be incorporated into baking better if they are used at room temperature. This takes about 45 minutes once they have been removed from the refrigerator.

6 Grated cheddar and other hard-style cheeses can be kept in well-sealed packets in the freezer to use. Just add a handful to a sauce and stir in, or scatter onto toast and grill.

7 Do not boil cheese once it has been stirred into a sauce or soup. Cheese is a high-protein food and when boiled or overcooked it toughens and goes stringy.

8 Use medium-fat cheeses like edam or gruyère for cheese on toast. They will not run over the edges of the toast as a cheddar will.

9 Cheese is best kept wrapped in a cloth or clean Chux in a cool place like a cellar where there is good air flow, at around 10°C. However, most of us do not have this luxury so the vegetable crisper in the fridge is the next best option. Have the cheese well wrapped in a cloth or greaseproof paper and then loosely in plastic wrap. Always allow cheese to come to room temperature before serving.

10 Cheese is a living product, so if it forms mould it is perfectly all right, as long as you cut away and discard any mouldy pieces. Most of our cheeses are sold with a 'Best By' date on them. This does not mean that they are 'off' the following day, it simply means that the cheese will be at its best for eating at around this date. It can be kept longer if wished — the choice is yours.

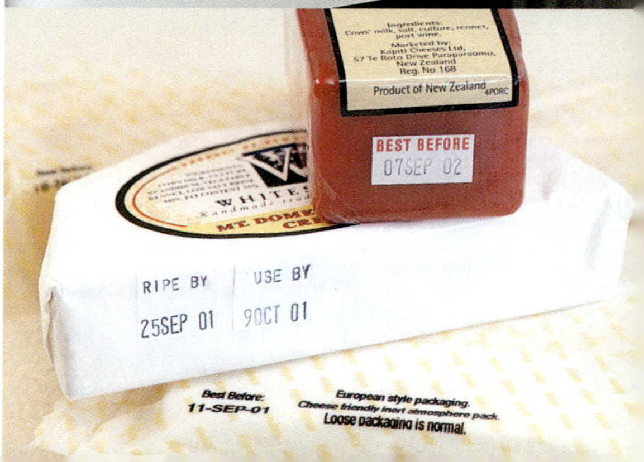

sweet indian curried eggs

6–8 eggs
1 red onion, peeled and diced
1 tblsp oil
1 apple, grated

415 gram can **Wattie's Tikka Masala Curry Sauce**
2 tblsp plain, unsweetened yoghurt, or use cream
salt
chopped fresh parsley or coriander to garnish (optional)

1. Place the eggs in water and bring quickly to the boil. Boil for 8 minutes. Pour off the water, crack the shells and then plunge into cold water. When cool enough to handle, peel.
2. Cook the onion in the oil in a hot frying pan for 3–5 minutes until the onion has softened.
3. Add the apple and curry sauce. Simmer uncovered for 5 minutes. Stir in the yoghurt or cream. Season with salt.
4. Halve the eggs and fold into the curry sauce. Serve over rice or noodles, garnished with parsley or coriander if wished.

Serves 3–4

variation

- Add ¼ cup chopped raisins with the apple if wished. Use a grated pear or nashi instead of the apple.

thai curried eggs on noodles

6–8 eggs
1 small onion, peeled and finely diced
1 tblsp oil
2 tblsp Thai flavour base*
½ cup coconut cream or milk
2 tblsp **Eta Peanut Butter**
2 tblsp chopped fresh coriander, mint or parsley
2–4 tblsp chopped toasted peanuts
salt and pepper and fish sauce for seasoning
extra finely sliced mint or coriander for garnish

1. Put the eggs in water and bring them quickly to the boil. Boil for 8 minutes, pour off the water, crack the shells and plunge into cold water. When cool enough to handle, peel. Set aside.
2. Cook the onion in the oil in a hot frying pan for 3–5 minutes until softened.
3. Add the Thai flavour base and cook for a further minute. Stir in the coconut cream or milk and peanut butter. Simmer for 5 minutes.
4. Cut the eggs in half and fold through the curry with the herbs and peanuts. Season with salt and pepper and a dash of fish sauce.
5. Serve over noodles tossed with pan-fried greens like beans or bok choy. Sprinkle over extra sliced mint or coriander to garnish.

Serves 4

Use any prepared, store-purchased Thai flavour base.

kedgeree

1 onion, peeled and diced
2 tblsp oil
2 tsp minced garlic
2 tsp minced ginger
1 tblsp spicy curry powder or paste
1 tsp salt
2 cups long-grain rice (Basmati is lovely here)
3 cups vegetable or chicken stock
1 apple, peeled and grated
1 bay leaf (optional)
2 cups frozen **Wattie's Freshlock™ Mixed Vegetables**
4 freshly cooked hard-boiled eggs
180 gram can **Greenseas Tuna in Oil**, well drained
2 tblsp chopped fresh coriander or parsley

1. In a heavy-based saucepan, cook the onion in the oil for 3–5 minutes until softened.
2. Add the garlic, ginger, curry powder or paste and salt and cook for a further minute.
3. Add the rice and turn in the hot oil for 1 minute or until the rice becomes white. Pour in the stock and stir in the grated apple and bay leaf.
4. Cover and simmer slowly for 10 minutes. Add the frozen vegetables and then continue to cook for a further 5 minutes. Remove from the heat, but do not lift the lid. Allow the rice to stand for a further 5 minutes.
5. Cut the eggs into quarters. Toss the eggs, tuna and herbs through the rice and serve immediately.

Serves 4

top sweet indian curried eggs
bottom thai curried eggs on noodles

basic pancake

½ cup flour
pinch salt
1 egg
¾ cup milk
knob of butter

1. Sift the flour and salt into a bowl and make a well in the centre. Beat the egg and milk together and slowly pour into the well, gradually mixing with a wooden spoon to form a thin, smooth batter. If lumpy, strain the batter.
2. Cover and stand for 30 minutes. This softens the gluten in the flour and ensures a lighter batter.
3. Heat a small knob of butter in a pancake pan and when sizzling, pour in about a ½ ladle of batter, turning the pancake pan so the base is evenly coated.
4. Cook for about 2 minutes until the base of the pancake browns and the top begins to dry. Quickly flip the pancake and cook for a further minute. Set aside on a plate, covered with a clean towel, while you cook the remaining pancakes.

Makes **6–8**

mushroom and ham pancakes

1 quantity Basic Pancakes (see above)
1 onion, peeled and diced
1 tsp minced garlic
2 tblsp butter
3 tblsp flour
1½ cups milk
220 gram can **Wattie's Sliced Mushrooms in Peppercorn Sauce**
100 grams sliced, shredded ham
2 tblsp chopped chives
¾ cup grated cheese

1. Cook the onion and garlic in the butter over a low-moderate heat for 5–7 minutes until softened. Stir in the flour and cook for 1–2 minutes until frothy.
2. Gradually stir in the milk and cook, stirring regularly, until the sauce thickens. Add the mushrooms, ham and chives.
3. Place 1 pancake on a heatproof serving dish. Spread with a little of the sauce. Top with more sauce and then another pancake. Continue in this fashion, finishing with a pancake on top. Sprinkle over the cheese.
4. Bake at 200°C for 15 minutes until hot and golden.

Serves **4**

asparagus and crème fraîche pancakes

1 quantity Basic Pancakes (see page 26)
1 onion, peeled and sliced
2 tblsp butter
3 tblsp flour
1 cup milk
250 gram tub Tararua Crème Fraîche
2 tblsp chopped fresh herbs (tarragon, chives, parsley, dill)

salt and pepper to season
340 gram can **Wattie's Asparagus Spears**, well drained
¼ cup white wine
1 tsp prepared mustard (Dijon is nice here)
½ cup grated parmesan cheese
1 tblsp chopped fresh herbs for garnish

1 Cook the pancakes and have them ready.

2 Cook the onion in the butter for 3–5 minutes until softened. Stir in the flour and cook for 1 minute. Slowly add the milk and cook, stirring, until the sauce thickens. Stir in the crème fraîche and herbs. Season with salt and pepper.

3 Using half the cream mixture, take 1 pancake and place 2 tablespoons of the mixture at the top and spread out evenly. Arrange 2–3 spears of asparagus on top and roll up. Repeat with the remaining ingredients. Place in a lasagne-style dish.

4 Reheat the remaining filling, adding the wine and mustard. Pour over the pancakes and sprinkle with the grated cheese.

5 Bake at 200°C for 15 minutes. Sprinkle with chopped herbs before serving.

Serves 4

basic tart pastry

1½ cups flour
½ tsp salt
150 grams butter, chilled and diced
2 egg yolks
1–2 tblsp chilled water

to make by hand

1. Sift the flour and salt into a bowl.
2. Using your fingertips, rub in the butter until the mixture resembles fine crumbs.
3. Use a knife and cut in the egg yolks and sufficient water until the pastry begins to form large clumps, so that when a small portion is gathered in the hand and pressed, it will stay together.
4. Turn the dough out and bring together. Wrap in greaseproof paper and refrigerate for 1 hour before using.

food processor method

1. Place the flour, salt and butter in a food processor fitted with a metal blade and process until the mixture resembles fine crumbs.
2. Pulse in the egg yolks and sufficient water until the mixture forms moist balls of dough. Sufficient water has been added when you can gather a small amount of the mixture in your hand and press it together to form a larger mass that holds its shape.
3. Turn out and bring together, kneading only lightly. Wrap in greaseproof paper and refrigerate for 1 hour before using.

Makes 350 grams pastry

bacon and tuna tart

1 quantity Basic Tart Pastry*
2–3 rashers lean bacon, finely diced
180 gram can **Greenseas Tuna in Oil**, well drained
1 cup finely grated cheese (try gruyère)
1 tblsp finely chopped fresh sage or oregano
4 eggs
1 cup cream or whole milk
salt and pepper to season
1 sliced tomato to garnish (optional)

1. Roll the pastry out to line the base and sides of a 24 cm, loose-bottom, metal flan tin. Trim away excess pastry and press the edges firmly. Prick the base of the tart evenly all over with a fork.
2. Line with baking paper and fill the centre with an even layer of baking blind material (ceramic beans/dried pulses).
3. Bake at 200°C for 12 minutes or until the edge is beginning to colour. Remove the baking blind material and paper and return the pastry shell to the oven for a further 5–7 minutes or until the pastry is cooked.
4. Scatter over the bacon, tuna, cheese and herbs. Beat the eggs and cream or milk together and season well with salt and pepper. Pour carefully over the bacon, tuna and cheese.
5. Bake at 190°C for 30 minutes or until the filling is set and golden. Serve garnished with sliced tomato if using.

Serves 6

For a short cut, in place of making your own pastry, use a 400 gram block of frozen savoury pastry (defrosted), or 2 sheets of pre-rolled savoury pastry, rolled together.

corn and asparagus tart

1 prepared flan (see Bacon and Tuna Tart)
3 eggs
3 spring onions, trimmed and finely chopped
¾ cup grated cheese
½ cup cream
1 cup milk
425 gram can **Wattie's Whole Kernel Corn**, well drained
340 gram can **Wattie's Asparagus Spears**, well drained

1. Prepare the pastry flan base as for the Bacon and Tuna Tart. See points 1–3.
2. In a bowl mix together the eggs, spring onion, ½ cup of the grated cheese, cream, milk and corn. Pour in the filling.
3. Arrange the asparagus spears on top and sprinkle over the remaining ¼ cup grated cheese.
4. Bake at 180°C for about 40 minutes until the filling is golden and set.

Serves 6

top bacon and tuna tart
bottom corn and asparagus tart

basic omelette

6 eggs
salt and pepper to season
oil or butter for pan-frying

1. Crack the eggs into a bowl. Season well with salt and pepper and beat well with a fork. Heat about a teaspoon of oil or butter in a frying pan or omelette pan and when hot pour in half the mixture.

2. Using the fork, move the egg mix quickly around the pan until it begins to cook. Once this happens, stop stirring.

3. When the top of the omelette is almost cooked through, roll over and turn out onto a plate to serve immediatley.

Makes 2

omelette filling ideas
asparagus, ham and cheese
When the omelette is nearly cooked, fill with a few **Wattie's Asparagus Spears** and a little ham and cheese in the centre, fold over and serve.

mushroom, herb and cheese
When the omelette is nearly cooked, fill the centre with sliced **Wattie's Whole Mushrooms in Brine**, your favourite herbs and cheese and fold to serve.

thai-flavoured noodle cakes

2 packets **Wattie's Spicy Chicken 99% Fat Free Noodles**
2 tblsp **Wattie's Asian Chilli Sauce**
4 eggs
2–3 spring onions, trimmed and finely chopped
1–2 tblsp chopped fresh coriander
1–2 tblsp chopped fresh parsley
2 tsp each minced ginger and garlic
2 tsp chopped lemon grass (optional)
butter or oil for pan-frying

1. Pour 4 cups boiling water over the noodles, including the flavour sachet, and allow to stand for 2–3 minutes. Break the noodle cake up with a fork as it stands.

2. Drain well and cut the noodles randomly with scissors and place in a bowl. Add the chilli sauce, eggs, spring onion, herbs, ginger, garlic and lemon grass and mix well to combine.

3. Cook large spoonfuls of noodles in the hot oil in a frying pan for 2–3 minutes and when brown underneath, flip and cook the second side for a further 2 minutes.

4. Serve the noodle cakes with chilli sauce.

Makes 10–12

creamy spinach macaroni

creamy spinach macaroni
4 cups macaroni
boiling, salted water
250 gram packet frozen **Wattie's Freshlock™ Chopped Spinach**, drained
¼ cup cream cheese
salt, pepper and grated nutmeg to season

cheese sauce
50 grams butter
4 tblsp flour
2 cups milk
1 cup grated cheddar cheese
salt, pepper and grated nutmeg to season

topping (optional)
½ cup dry breadcrumbs
1 cup grated cheddar cheese

1. Cook the macaroni in boiling, salted water until 'al dente', then drain.
2. Mix the spinach and cream cheese together, seasoning well with salt, pepper and nutmeg.
3. Prepare the cheese sauce. Heat the butter in a saucepan and add the flour. Cook for 2 minutes until frothy. Gradually stir in the milk and cook until thickened. Stir in the grated cheese and season with salt and pepper and a pinch of nutmeg.
4. Toss the macaroni into the cheese sauce and stir to mix.
5. Arrange half the macaroni in a 6-cup-capacity, greased lasagne-style dish. Spread the spinach on top. Cover with the remaining macaroni mixture.
6. Sprinkle over the breadcrumbs and cheese if using. Bake at 180°C for 35–40 minutes until hot and golden. Serve with salad.

Serves **4–5**

quick lemon tuna soufflé

150 gram pouch **Greenseas Lemon and Cracked Pepper Tuna**
4 large eggs, separated
1 small onion, peeled and chopped
3 slices white toast bread, crusts removed
½ tsp salt
1 tblsp chopped fresh parsley
1 cup milk
25 grams softened butter
2 tblsp dry breadcrumbs

1. Put the tuna, egg yolks, onion, bread, salt and parsley into a food processor and process until well chopped and smooth.
2. Add the milk and butter and pulse to blend.
3. In a clean bowl, beat the egg whites until they form soft peaks (the egg whites should still be shiny, not dry).
4. Fold the tuna mixture into the egg whites.
5. Turn into a well-greased and lightly breadcrumb-dusted, 4-cup-capacity, soufflé dish.
6. Bake at 180°C for 35–40 minutes until well risen and golden on top. The centre should be slightly undercooked. Serve immediately with salad.

Serves 4

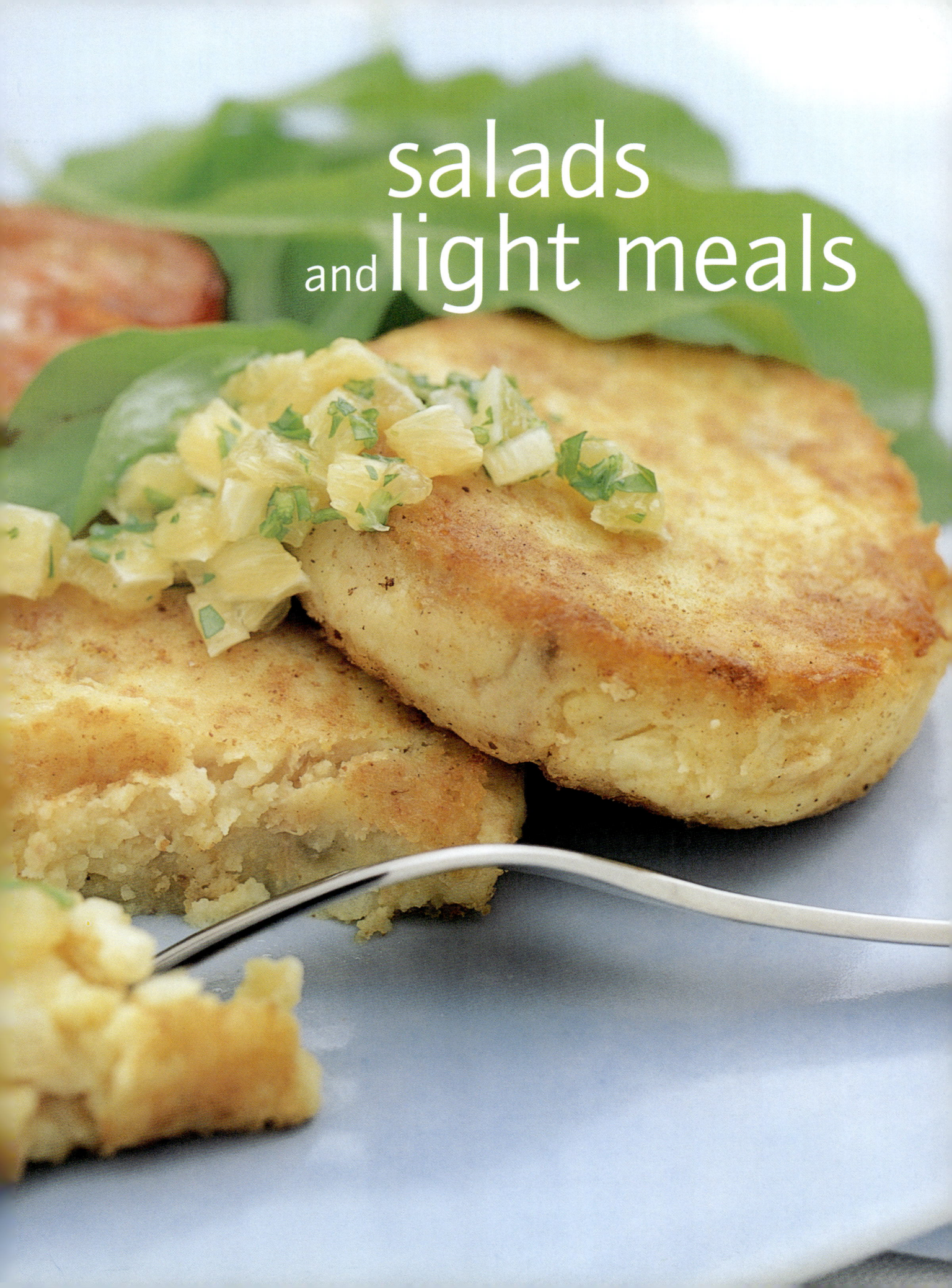
salads and light meals

{salads and light meals}
tips and hints

1

1 Leftover Wattie's tomato paste can be frozen in ice cubes. Once frozen, transfer to a snaplock or freezer bag for easy storage and handling. One ice cube is about 1 heaped tablespoon.

2 When buying prepared minced garlics, look for those that are well sealed and are not brown, as this means they have oxidised and will have off-flavours. Once opened, keep refrigerated and use quickly. Each brand varies, so find your favourite.

2

3 To keep cut herbs longer, rinse them under cold water and shake dry. Place in a snaplock or similar bag, blow up lightly with your own breath and seal; keep refrigerated. Repeat this every second day and wash before chopping.

4 When we cut herbs on a chopping board, some essential oils are lost to the chopping board. If you can, cut with scissors.

3

4

5 Do not keep fresh tomatoes in the fridge: they are a fruit, so keep them in a cool area away from heat and light. This way they will continue their natural ripening. The majority of New Zealand tomatoes are not sprayed with pesticides and all are vine-ripened.

6 Keep spices well sealed, away from light, heat and moisture. Once a bottle or packet of spices is opened it will loose valuable essential oils. After six months of being opened the spices should be replaced as they lose their intense flavour.

7 Choosing the right olive oil can be daunting — there are so many brands and varieties. Extra virgin olive oil is cold pressed oil with an acidity of less than 1 percent and is ideal for salads or wherever you will taste it. Virgin or fine virgin olive oils are also cold pressed or crushed and have an acidity of less than 2 percent — great for making your own mayonnaise or dressings.

Olive oil and pure olive oil are extracted under heat and are ideal for cooking. Light olive oil is a blend of refined olive oil and virgin olive oils; it is light in flavour and carries the same amount of calories as any other olive oil.

8 Our humble Wattie's baked beans make a great instant meal. For the record, they are high in fibre and protein, low in fat and you can also buy a low-salt variant. Keep them on hand in the pantry.

9 If your nacho chips have softened in the pantry, place them in a single layer on a baking tray and reheat at 150°C for 10–12 minutes until crispy again.

10 The more you chop garlic, the stronger its flavour: chopping releases more essential oils. If you want a light garlic flavour in your salad, rub the cut half of a garlic clove around the bowl. For a stronger flavour, finely chop the garlic and add to the dressing.

cheat's soufflé

about 25 grams butter
10 slices white bread
4 rashers bacon, cooked until crisp
4 eggs
420 gram can **Wattie's Cream Style Corn**
2 cups milk
½ cup grated cheddar cheese
chopped parsley to garnish (optional)

1. Butter the bread slices and sandwich together to make 5 sandwiches. Trim the crusts from each and cut into quarters.
2. Arrange the bread randomly in a 2 litre, ovenproof dish. Crumble the bacon and scatter over the bread.
3. In a large bowl or jug beat together the eggs, corn and milk. Pour over the bread evenly and then sprinkle over the grated cheese.
4. Fan-bake at 180°C (or 200°C bake) for 30 minutes. Serve hot, garnished with chopped parsley, if wished.

Serves 4

variations

- Add 1–2 tblsp wholeseed mustard.
- Add 2–3 tblsp chopped, fresh parsley.
- Add 100 grams crumbled feta.
- Use crispy, pan-fried salami instead of bacon.

made-in-one-pan dinner

1 onion, peeled and diced
500 grams Quality Mark Lean, Minced Beef
2 tblsp oil
1 large, golden kumara, peeled and diced
2 tsp Marmite (or use Vegemite or Promite)
1 tblsp flour
½ cup **Wattie's Tomato Sauce**
1½ cups water or beef stock
½ 750 gram bag frozen **Wattie's Freshlock™ Chuckwagon Corn**

1. Cook the onion and mince in the oil in a large, lidded frying pan for 4–5 minutes over a high heat until the onion has softened and the mince is browned. Break up the mince with the back of a wooden spoon or a fork as you go. It is best to do this in two batches, otherwise the mince may stew rather than brown. Stir in the kumara.
2. In a jug mix together the Marmite, flour, tomato sauce and water and pour over the mince. Cover and simmer gently for 10–15 minutes until the kumara is almost cooked.
3. Add the corn mix and stir. Cover and simmer for a further 10 minutes. Season if wished.

Serves 4

boston baked beans

4 pork slices, rind removed
dash oil
2 onions, peeled and finely chopped
1–2 tsp minced garlic
1 tblsp dry mustard
2 tblsp brown sugar
¼ cup golden syrup
2 x 420 gram cans **Wattie's Baked Beans**
¼ cup **Lea & Perrins Worcestershire Sauce**
¼ cup **Wattie's Tomato Sauce**
chopped parsley to garnish (optional)

1. Cut the pork into 1 cm-wide pieces. Heat the oil in a large, heatproof casserole and cook the pork over a moderate heat until well browned.
2. Add the onion and garlic and cook for a further 2 minutes.
3. Add the mustard, brown sugar, golden syrup, baked beans, Worcestershire sauce and tomato sauce.
4. Stir, cover and simmer gently for about 10 minutes.
5. Serve hot on toast or English muffins for brunch or with green vegetables for dinner. Garnish with chopped parsley, if wished, before serving.

Serves 4

a

b

c

chicken and chilli bean enchiladas

enchiladas
1 tblsp oil
500 grams chicken breast, sliced finely
1 tsp minced garlic
1 carrot, peeled and grated
400 gram can **Wattie's Mexican Spiced Tomatoes**
425 gram can **Craig's Chilli Beans**
10 enchilada tortillas
3/4–1 cup grated cheese

avocado salsa
1 avocado, halved, stoned, peeled and diced
2 tblsp chopped coriander or parsley
2 tblsp lemon juice
salt and pepper to season
sour cream to accompany

enchiladas
1 Heat the oil and cook the chicken for 2–3 minutes, until lightly browned. Add the garlic and carrot and cook for a further 1 minute. (a)

2 Add the tomatoes and beans and simmer for 5 minutes or until the chicken is cooked. (b)

3 Take one enchilada tortilla and fill with a large spoonful of the mixture. Roll up tightly to enclose and place in a greased, lasagne-style dish. Spoon over any remaining sauce. Sprinkle with grated cheese. (c)

4 Bake at 180°C for 20 minutes until hot and golden.

5 Serve with the Avocado Salsa and sour cream.

avocado salsa
1 Toss together the diced avocado, coriander or parsley, lemon juice and salt and pepper to season.

Serves 4–5

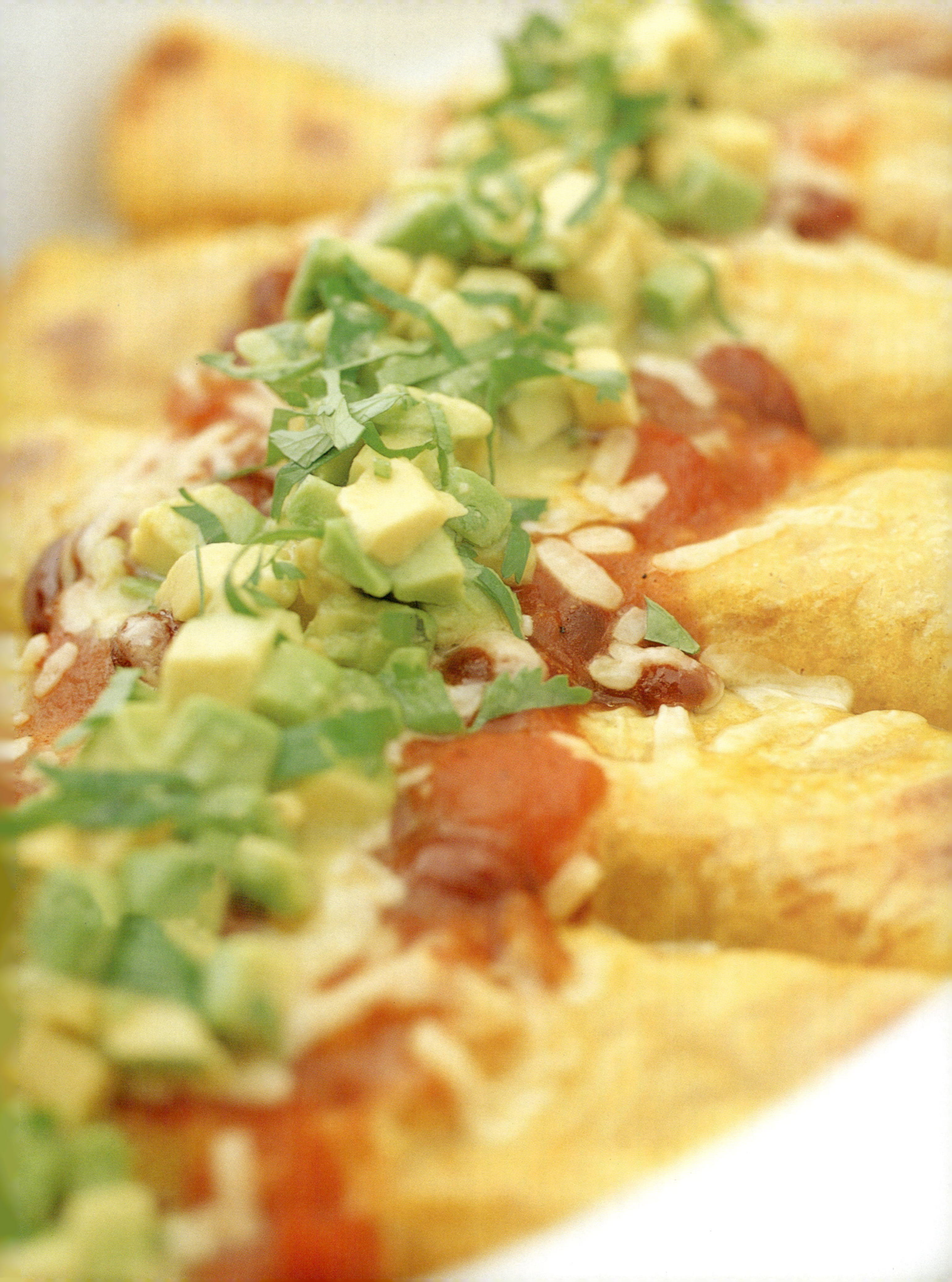

smoked honey chicken salad

125 grams rice vermicelli
1 **Tegel Honey Smoked Chicken Breast**
1 telegraph cucumber, halved
1 carrot, peeled and cut into thin match sticks
½ cup chopped fresh mint
¼ cup chopped fresh coriander or parsley
2–3 tsp each minced chilli and ginger
½ cup **Good Taste Company Lime and Dill Salad Dressing**
½ cup honey roasted peanuts (optional)

1. Cook the rice vermicelli noodles in boiling, salted water for 4–5 minutes. Drain thoroughly and then cut randomly.
2. Finely slice the chicken. Deseed the cucumber and then cut on an angle into thin slices.
3. In a bowl, toss together the noodles, chicken, cucumber, carrot, mint, coriander (or parsley), chilli, ginger and dressing.
4. Serve in bowls garnished with the peanuts if wished.

Serves 4

mexican potato salad

500 grams baby potatoes, well washed
4 rashers rindless bacon, chopped
1–2 tblsp oil
1–2 avocados, halved, stoned and peeled
2 tomatoes, chopped
4 spring onions, trimmed and sliced
300 gram can **Wattie's Whole Kernel Corn**, well drained
½ cup **Eta Potato Salad Dressing**
1–2 tsp Tabasco sauce
juice 1 lemon

1. Cook the baby potatoes in plenty of boiling, salted water until tender. Drain well. Cool and halve.
2. Cook the bacon in the oil in a hot pan until crisp. Drain on absorbent paper. Dice the avocado.
3. In a bowl toss together gently the potatoes, bacon, avocado, tomatoes, spring onion, corn, salad dressing, Tabasco sauce and lemon juice. Season with salt and pepper if wished.

Serves 4–6

french salad

salad
- 500 gram packet frozen **Wattie's Freshlock™ Broad Beans** (optional)
- ½ 750 gram packet frozen **Wattie's Freshlock™ Whole Baby Green Beans**
- 1 lettuce (iceberg is fine)
- 4 tomatoes, cut into eighths
- 10 cooked baby potatoes, halved
- 4 hard-boiled eggs, peeled
- 180 gram can **Greenseas Tuna in Spring Water**
- 12 black olives (optional)

dressing
- ½ cup **Wattie's Mayonnaise**
- ¼ cup chopped, fresh herbs (parsley, chives, chervil or basil)
- 2 tblsp water

salad
1 Blanch the broad and baby beans in boiling water for 2 minutes. Refresh in cold water and drain well. Peel the broad beans.
2 Wash and drain the lettuce. Cut into large pieces and arrange on a serving platter.
3 Sprinkle over half the whole baby and broad beans. Top with the tomatoes and potatoes.
4 Halve the hard-boiled eggs and place on top. Sprinkle over the remaining whole baby and broad beans.
5 Drain the tuna and flake on top of the salad. Lastly, scatter over the olives.

dressing
1 Stir all the dressing ingredients together until smooth and spoon over just before serving.

Serves 5–6

noodle crab cakes

2 packets **Wattie's Spicy Chicken 99% Fat Free Noodles**
170 gram can crabmeat, well drained
4 eggs
2 tblsp chopped coriander or parsley
½ tsp minced ginger
½ tsp minced garlic
salt and pepper to season

1. Pour boiling water to cover the noodles and the flavour sachets and stand for 2 minutes. Drain and chop the noodles roughly.
2. In a bowl, toss together the noodles, crabmeat, eggs, coriander or parsley, ginger and garlic. Season with salt and pepper.
3. Heat a little oil in a frying pan and cook tablespoonfuls of noodles. When golden crispy underneath, flip and cook for a further minute or two.
4. Keep warm in a low oven while cooking the remaining mix. Serve the fritters with the Asian Guacamole.

asian guacamole

2 avocados, diced
1 tsp minced fresh chilli
1 tblsp each chopped fresh mint and coriander or parsley
2 tblsp honey
1 tblsp sesame oil

1. Mix all ingredients together in a bowl and toss together.

Serves **4**

baked bean hash

500 gram packet frozen **Wattie's Hash Browns**
420 gram can **Wattie's Baked Beans**
4 eggs
4 rashers bacon
¾ cup grated cheese (edam, cheddar or gouda)
freshly ground black pepper to season (optional)
chopped parsley to garnish (optional)

1. Place the hash browns in the base of a dish approximately 16 cm x 26 cm, trimming the hash browns where necessary to fit.
2. Pour over the baked beans and level out.
3. Beat the eggs together and pour over the top of the baked beans.
4. Finely slice the bacon and sprinkle on top of the eggs. Sprinkle over the grated cheese and season with pepper if wished.
5. Bake at 200°C towards the top of the oven for 30 minutes, until the eggs have set. Stand for 2 minutes before cutting into squares to serve. Sprinkle with the chopped parsley if using. Serve in wedges.

Serves **4**

big eat tart

2 cups self-raising flour
25 grams butter
1 cup grated, tasty cheddar cheese
2 tblsp chopped fresh thyme or parsley
¾ cup milk

410 gram can **Wattie's Big Eat Spicy Chilli Beans**
1 courgette, trimmed and grated
2–4 tblsp finely chopped black olives (optional)
milk to glaze
chopped parsley to garnish (optional)

1. Sift the flour into a bowl and rub in the butter until the mixture resembles fine crumbs. Stir in half the grated cheese and the thyme or parsley.

2. Stir in the milk to form a soft dough. Turn out and knead lightly on a floured board until smooth.

3. Roll the dough out to about a 30 cm-diameter circle. Place the dough over the base and sides of a 24 cm metal flan or cake tin, allowing the edges to overhang.

4. Combine the chilli beans, courgette and olives and pile into the scone-lined tin. Flip the edges over and brush with milk to glaze. Sprinkle the remaining grated cheese over the top.

5. Bake at 200°C for 20–25 minutes, or until hot and golden and the scone dough is well risen and golden.

6. Sprinkle with chopped parsley to garnish before serving.

Serves 4

classic fish cakes

4 large starchy potatoes, peeled and quartered
hearty knob butter
½ onion, finely chopped or minced
1–2 tsp curry powder
2 x 180 gram cans **Greenseas Tuna in Oil** or **Springwater**, well drained
1 egg
clarified butter or oil for pan-frying

parsley and lemon toss (optional)
1 lemon
2 tblsp chopped fresh parsley

fish cakes

1 Cook the potatoes in boiling, salted water for about 15 minutes until tender. Drain well and mash with the knob of butter.
2 Add the onion and curry powder and then flake in the tuna. Add the egg and mix well with a fork, but try to keep some largish pieces of tuna in the mixture.
3 Dust your hands with flour and mould the mixture into 8 even-sized and shaped patties.
4 Heat the clarified butter in a frying pan and cook the tuna cakes over a moderate heat for 5 minutes on each side until golden and heated through. Serve with grilled tomatoes, a fresh salad, or the Parsely and Lemon Toss if wished.

parsely and lemon toss
1 Finely dice the flesh of one lemon and mix with the parsley.

Serves 4–6

variations
- Use kumara or pumpkin instead of potatoes.
- Add finely chopped herbs such as parsley, chives, or even mint.

vegetarian nachos

700 gram packet **Wattie's Crunchy Wedges**
2 tblsp oil
1 onion, peeled and finely chopped
600–700 grams pumpkin, finely diced or coarsely grated
300 gram jar **Wattie's Bit On the Side Tomato Tango Salsa**
½ cup water
¼ cup chopped fresh parsley or coriander
¼ cup chopped stuffed olives (optional)
1 cup grated cheese

extra toppings (optional)
sour cream
diced avocado
chopped fresh coriander or parsley for garnish

1 Bake the wedges at 230°C for 10 minutes.
2 Heat the oil in a frying pan and cook the onion and pumpkin for about 5 minutes, stirring regularly.
3 Add the tomato salsa, water, parsley or coriander and olives, if using. Stir, cover and simmer for about 15 minutes until the pumpkin is soft.
4 Arrange the crispy wedges on a heatproof plate. Spoon over the pumpkin topping and sprinkle over the grated cheese.
5 Grill under a high heat for about 5 minutes until the cheese is golden.
6 To serve, top with sour cream, diced avocado and chopped coriander or parsley if wished.

Serves 4

quick and easy nachos

nachos
1 onion, peeled and finely chopped
1 tblsp oil
425 gram can **Craig's Spicy Mexican Beans**
3 medium-sized tomatoes, diced
340 gram can **Hellaby's Corned Beef**
your favourite nacho chips

topping
1 avocado, halved and stoned
1 spring onion, peeled and finely sliced
1 tblsp chopped fresh coriander or parsley
juice 1 lemon
sour cream to accompany

1 Cook the onion in the oil in a frying pan for about 5 minutes until well softened.
2 Add the beans and tomatoes and simmer gently for 5 minutes. Dice the corned beef, add to the beans and heat through.
3 Dice the avocado and mix with the spring onion, coriander or parsley and lemon juice.
4 Arrange 1 packet of your favourite nacho chips on a serving plate and spread the bean sauce on top. Arrange the avocado mixture on top of the nachos and garnish with sour cream.

Serves 4

classic fish cakes

tropical baked kumara

4 medium-sized orange or golden kumara
dash oil
½ cup well-drained crushed pineapple
1 tsp minced fresh ginger (optional)
2–3 spring onions, trimmed and chopped
340 gram can **Hellaby's Corned Beef**
¼–½ cup grated cheese

1. Wash the kumara and dry well. Trim the ends. Rub the kumara with oil and place on a baking tray. Cook at 200°C for 45–50 minutes or until tender. Alternatively, prick the kumara with a fork and microwave on high power for 15 minutes or until tender.
2. Slice a top off each kumara and scoop the flesh into a bowl. Add the pineapple, ginger, spring onion and corned beef and mix gently with a fork to break up the corned beef and mix the ingredients lightly. Do not mash.
3. Re-fill the kumaras with the mixture and place on the baking tray. Sprinkle with grated cheese.
4. Cook at 200°C for 15 minutes until piping hot and golden.

Serves 4

sweet chilli corn fritters

2 cups self-raising flour
1 tsp baking powder
1 tsp ground cumin or coriander (optional)
salt and pepper to season
2 eggs
½ cup **Wattie's Bit on the Side Sweet Chilli Sauce**
½ cup water
2 cups frozen **Wattie's Freshlock™ Sweetcorn**
¼ cup chopped fresh coriander or parsley
butter for pan-frying

1. Sift the flour, baking powder, cumin or coriander, salt and pepper into a bowl, and make a well in the centre.
2. Mix together the eggs, chilli sauce, water, corn and coriander or parsley and stir gently into the flour.
3. Heat a knob of butter in a frying pan and when hot place 3–4 large spoonfuls of mixture in the pan. Once bubbles form on the top of the corn cakes, flip and cook the other side for a further 2 minutes or until cooked and tender.
4. Serve with grilled bacon, sliced avocado and sour cream. Garnish with a sprig of fresh coriander or parsley.

Makes about 12

roasted tomato and bean salad

5–6 medium-sized juicy tomatoes, halved
salt, pepper and sugar to season
3–4 tblsp oil (olive is nice here)
8–10 small cloves garlic, peeled and thickly sliced
2 tblsp oil
1 tblsp cumin seeds

425 gram can **Craig's Mixed Bean Salad**, well drained
100–150 grams pastrami, thinly sliced
¼ cup fresh coriander leaves
¼ cup chopped fresh mint
2–3 tblsp lemon juice or vinegar
salt and pepper to season

1 Place the halved tomatoes in an ovenproof dish and season well with salt, pepper and a pinch of sugar. Drizzle with oil.
2 Bake at 200°C for 25 minutes.
3 Heat the garlic in the hot oil until light and just brown. Add the cumin seeds and remove from the heat. Cool.
4 Toss the cooled garlic and cumin scented oil together with the bean salad, pastrami, coriander, mint and lemon juice or vinegar. Season with salt and pepper.
5 Serve the bean salad over the warm tomatoes, garnished, if wished, with baby sprigs of mint.

Serves 4

asparagus slice

12 slices streaky bacon, rind removed
500 gram packet **Wattie's Potato Medallions**
2 eggs
125 grams cream cheese
½ cup cream
2 tblsp chopped fresh dill or parsley
340 gram can **Wattie's Asparagus Spears**, well drained

1 Stretch the bacon rashers with the back of a large cook's knife and use them to line the base of a 25 cm x 11 cm x 7 cm loaf tin. **(a)**

2 Defrost the potato medallions in the microwave for 3 minutes and then cut into 1–2 cm chunks.

3 In a bowl beat together the eggs, cream cheese, cream and dill or parsley. Fold in the chopped medallions. **(b)**

4 Place one third of the potato mixture into the loaf tin. Arrange half the asparagus spears on top and repeat these layers, ending with the potato mix. **(c)** Fold over any bacon ends. **(d)**

5 Bake at 200°C for 40 minutes.

6 Allow to stand for 10 minutes before turning out of the tin and slicing. Serve with your favourite salad ingredients.

Serves 4–6

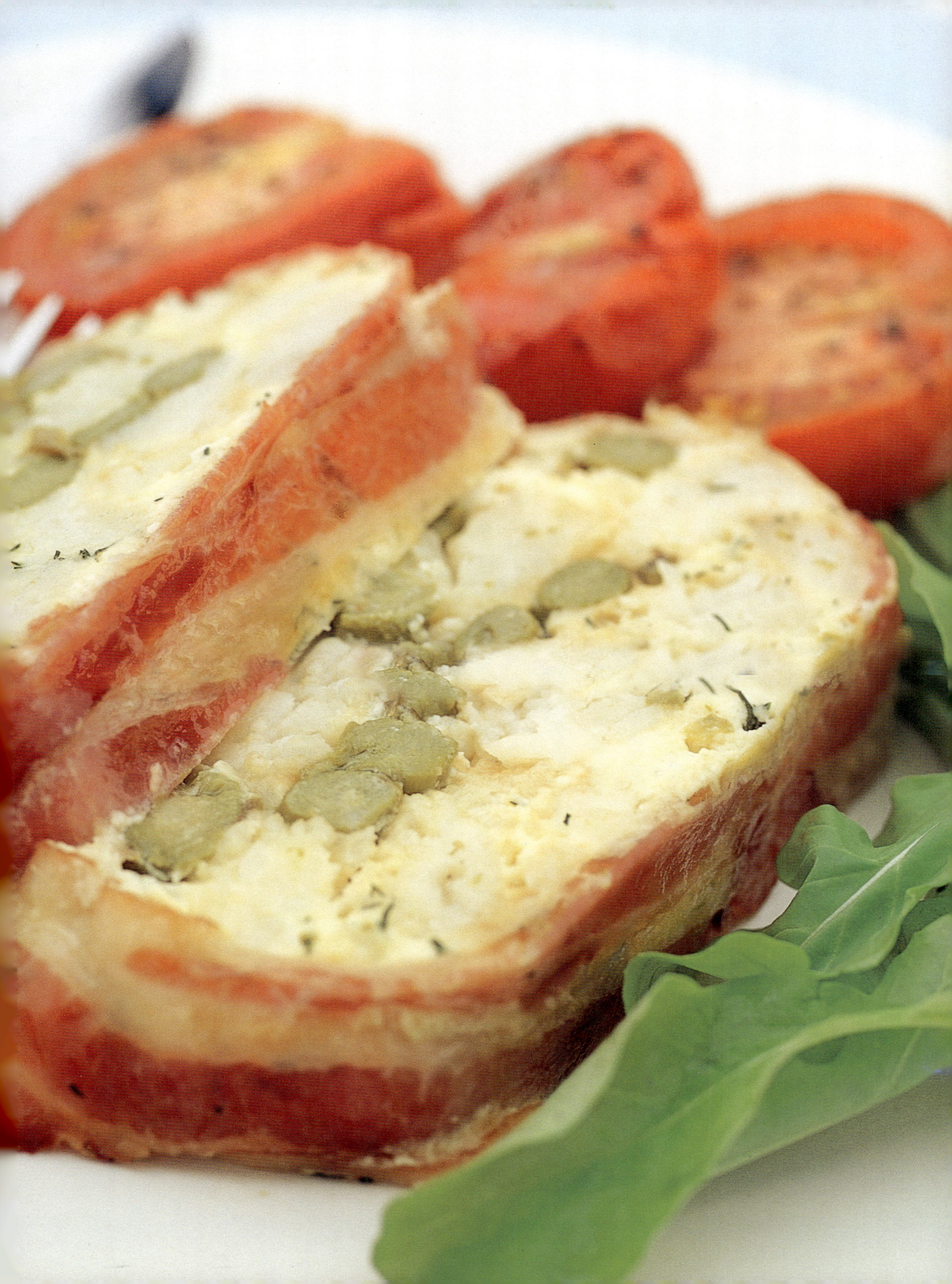

tropical rice salad

salad
- 2 litres water (8 cups)
- 2 tsp salt
- 1½ cups long-grain rice
- 1 Tegel Smoked Chicken
- 410 gram can **Wattie's Baby Corn Cuts in Brine**, well drained
- 1 cup chopped tropical fruit, like pawpaw, mangoes or pineapple
- 5–6 spring onions, trimmed and chopped
- 2–3 tsp minced ginger

dressing
- 1 cup **Wattie's Mayonnaise**
- ½ cup coconut milk
- grated rind and juice 2 large oranges

salad
1. Bring the water and salt to the boil. Sprinkle in the rice slowly and boil rapidly for 12 minutes. Drain through a colander and rinse with plenty of cold water to stop the cooking. Drain very well.
2. Pull the meat from the chicken and shred finely.
3. In a large bowl toss together the cooled rice, smoked chicken, corn, fruit, spring onion and ginger.

dressing
1. For the dressing mix together the mayonnaise, coconut milk, orange rind and juice and toss through.

Serves 6–8

grilled summer salad

salad
- 1 medium-sized aubergine
- 1 tblsp salt
- 1 red pepper, quartered and deseeded
- 1 yellow pepper, quartered and deseeded
- 4 courgettes, trimmed and halved
- oil for brushing
- 250 grams green or yellow beans, trimmed
- 1 punnet baby tomatoes, washed
- 6 flat mushrooms, thickly sliced

dressing
- ½ cup **Good Taste Company Italian Balsamic Vinaigrette**
- 2 tblsp each chopped chives and parsley

salad
1. Cut the aubergine into 0.5 cm slices, layer in a colander, sprinkling each layer with some of the salt and set aside for 30 minutes. Rinse well under cold water and pat dry on absorbent paper.
2. Brush all the vegetables with oil, place on a hot barbecue and cook quickly over a high heat. The vegetables will blacken, but in doing so become quite sweet.
3. Arrange the vegetables on a platter and pour over the dressing. Serve warm.

dressing
1. Stir the ingredients together.

Serves 4

hot potato and bacon salad

750 grams gourmet potatoes
1 red onion, cut into quarters
2 tblsp oil
4–6 rashers bacon
½ cup **Eta Creamy Pesto Dressing**

2 tblsp chopped fresh mint
2 spring onions, trimmed and sliced
1 tblsp sesame seeds, preferably toasted
salt and pepper to season

1. Rub the potatoes and onion in the oil and roast at 200°C for 35–40 minutes until cooked. (If the potatoes are large, halve before cooking.)
2. Grill or pan-fry the bacon until crispy. Crumble.
3. Place the potatoes, onion and bacon in a bowl and toss with the dressing, mint, spring onion and sesame seeds. Season with salt and pepper if wished.

Serves 4

tomato bean hot pot

1 onion, peeled and finely chopped
200 grams sliced or shaved ham
2 x 420 gram cans **Wattie's Chunky Tomato Baked Beans**
750 grams potatoes or kumara, peeled and cooked in boiling, salted water
milk and butter for mashing
1 cup grated cheese (gruyère, edam or cheddar)

1. Scatter the onion and sliced ham over the base of a 6-cup-capacity ovenproof dish.
2. Pour over the baked beans.
3. Mash the potatoes or kumara with milk and butter to suit and pile on top of the beans. Sprinkle with the grated cheese.
4. Bake at 200°C for 40 minutes until hot and golden. Serve with your favourite green vegetable.

Serves 4–5

baked bean boats

1–2 French sticks
420 gram can **Wattie's Baked Beans**
100 gram packet Brooks Italiano Salami, finely sliced
2 tomatoes, diced
4 spring onions, finely sliced
½ cup Mainland Grated Cheddar Cheese

1. Slice the French bread into 6–8 even-sized pieces and hollow out like a boat, leaving a 3 cm border around the edges. Bake at 200°C (fan-bake 180°C) for 3–5 minutes until warm.
2. Mix together the baked beans with the salami, tomato and spring onion. Fill the boats evenly with the filling and sprinkle with the grated cheddar cheese.
3. Fan-bake at 180°C for 10–12 minutes.

Serves 4

pasta and rice

{pasta and rice}
tips and hints

1 As a rule, thin sauces are tossed over thin-style pasta such as spaghetti, whereas chunky sauces are tossed through pastas like spirals, which can hold thicker sauces in their grooves.

2 Cook pasta in plenty of boiling salted water, stirring occasionally to prevent it sticking together. Allow 2.5 litres (10 cups) of water for every 200–250 grams of dried pasta.

3 Rice and pasta need salt; without it they'll lack flavour. Add it to the water when cooking. Allow about 1 tablespoon salt to every 4 litres water.

4 Allow 100–150 grams dried pasta per person. This is equivalent to 1–1½ cups dried macaroni or similar-style pasta.

5 Adding oil to the boiling water when cooking pasta does not really keep the grains or pasta separate – the oil floats to the top. It is best to toss the pasta in oil once drained. This is especially useful for pasta that is to be tossed in a salad.

6 When buying rice, look for whole grains. If the grains are broken or crushed, the rice is not the best and it will affect the quality of the finished dish.

7 There are many varieties of rice and each will need a different cooking time. To know when rice is cooked, take a grain and press it between your thumb and forefinger. If the grain is tender but not mushy, the rice is cooked. If it is still hard in the centre of the grain, continue cooking a little longer. Cooked rice should still have a little bite to it.

8 Rice absorbs lots of water as it cooks. If you are boiling rice, allow 6 cups water (boiling) to 1 cup rice. If you are cooking rice by the absorption method, as a rule of thumb allow 2½ cups water (boiling) for each 2 cups rice.

9 To cook rice in the microwave, place it in a very large, lidded, microwave-proof container. Pour over the right amount of water (2½ cups water to 2 cups rice), cover with a loose lid or plastic film and microwave on high power for 8 minutes. Stand for 5 minutes and then fluff with a fork.

10 Allow ½–¾ cup rice (uncooked) per person. Rice swells by three times its size when cooking, so your ½ cup becomes 1½ cups. This varies slightly with the different rice varieties.

creamy tomato sauce on fettuccini

1 onion, peeled and finely chopped
1 tblsp minced fresh garlic
3–4 tblsp oil
400 gram can **Wattie's Tomatoes in Seasoned Purée**
½ cup cream
1 tblsp cornflour
2–3 tblsp chopped fresh chives, basil or parsley
salt and pepper to season
fettuccini or spaghetti for two

1. Cook the onion and garlic in the oil over a low heat for about 5 minutes until soft and tender.
2. Roughly pulse the tomatoes in a food processor and add to the saucepan. Simmer gently for 5 minutes.
3. Mix the cream and cornflour together. Stir into the tomatoes and cook over a low heat until slightly thicker. Season with salt and pepper. Stir in the herbs.
4. Serve over fettuccini or spaghetti, garnished with crispy fried bacon, parmesan cheese and fresh herbs or chopped salami with olives if wished.

Serves 2

chicken and spinach cannelloni

2 cooked chicken breasts, diced
1 onion, peeled and finely chopped
1 tsp minced fresh garlic
250 gram packet frozen **Wattie's Freshlock™ Chopped Spinach**
½ cup cream
2 cups grated cheese
salt and pepper to season
400 gram packet fresh egg lasagne sheets
400 gram can **Wattie's Italian Seasoned** or **Pesto Style Tomatoes**

1. Toss together the chicken, onion, garlic, defrosted spinach, cream and half the grated cheese. Season.
2. Cut the lasagne sheets into 12 cm lengths and cook in boiling, salted water for 4–5 minutes until almost cooked. Drain.
3. Place 2–3 tblsp chicken mixture at one edge of a cooked piece of pasta and roll up to enclose. Repeat with the remaining pasta. Place in a lightly greased, ovenproof dish and pour over the tomatoes. Scatter over the remaining cheese.
4. Bake at 190°C for 40 minutes until hot and golden.

Serves 6

tortellini or ravioli with spinach cream

1 onion, peeled and diced
1–2 tsp minced garlic
2 tblsp oil
250 gram packet frozen **Wattie's Freshlock™ Chopped Spinach**, defrosted
½ cup cream
½–1 cup chicken or vegetable stock
½ cup grated parmesan cheese
salt and pepper to season
300 gram packet prepared chilled ravioli or tortellini

1 Cook the onion and garlic in the hot oil for 3 minutes until lightly brown.
2 Squeeze the spinach between two plates to remove excess moisture.
3 Add the spinach, cream, stock and parmesan cheese. Season with salt and pepper. Stir over a moderate heat until hot.
4 Cook the ravioli or tortellini according to the directions on the packet.
5 Drain and toss with the spinach sauce.
6 Serve in bowls garnished with extra grated parmesan cheese if wished.

Serves 2

variations
- Add 1 finely diced red pepper.
- Add 1–2 slices ham, finely diced.
- Add a few chopped olives or anchovies.
- Use spiral pasta in place of ravioli.

Pasta and Rice

aubergine cannelloni

1 aubergine
3–4 tblsp oil
1 cup cooked rice or orzo pasta
1 cup ricotta or cottage cheese
100 grams salami or cabana sausage, diced (optional)
about 2–3 tblsp chopped fresh herbs
400 gram can **Wattie's Pesto Style Tomatoes**
1 cup grated cheddar cheese

1. Cut aubergine lengthwise into long, thin strips. Brush with oil and pan-fry quickly until brown.

2. Mix together the rice or pasta, ricotta or cottage cheese, salami or cabana sausage (if using), herbs and half the tomatoes.

3. Place 2–3 tblsp of this mixture into each aubergine and roll up into a cylinder. Place in one layer in a lasagne-style dish and pour over the remaining tomato sauce. Scatter over the grated cheese.

4. Bake at 180°C for 35 minutes until the cheese is golden and the cannelloni hot. Serve with a green or tomato salad.

Serves 4

bahmi goreng

bahmi goreng

250 grams egg noodles
300 grams lean pork schnitzel, sliced
about 5 tblsp oil
1 tsp minced garlic
1 onion, peeled and finely diced
1 tsp minced ginger
1 stick celery, diced
150 grams cabbage, finely sliced

100 grams frozen **Wattie's Freshlock™ Whole Baby Green Beans**
4 spring onions, chopped
1 tblsp soy sauce

omelette (optional)

2 eggs
salt and pepper to season
2 tsp oil

bahmi goreng

1. Cook the noodles in a saucepan of boiling salted water for about 6 minutes. Drain and spread out to cool.

2. Heat 1 tablespoon oil in a wok or frying pan and cook the pork, garlic, onion, ginger, celery, cabbage and beans until lightly brown. Set aside.

3. Heat the remaining oil in the pan and cook the noodles over a high heat until pale and golden.

4. Return the pork mixture to the pan with the spring onion. Toss. Sprinkle with soy sauce. Serve in bowls as is or garnished with a finely sliced omelette.

omelette (optional)

1. Beat the eggs together lightly and season. Heat oil in a small pan and pour in the egg mixture. Cook until set. Remove, roll up and slice into thin strips.

Serves 4

sweetcorn and ricotta cheese sauce

300 grams lisci pasta (or use another shape)
25 grams butter
1 onion, chopped
2 stalks celery, finely sliced
2 rashers rindless bacon, diced
1 tblsp flour

½ cup vegetable stock
410 gram can **Wattie's Cream Style Corn**
200 gram tub ricotta
1–2 tblsp torn fresh basil leaves
salt and pepper to season
basil to garnish

1 Cook the lisci until 'al dente' then drain well.
2 Heat the butter in a saucepan and cook the onion, celery and bacon until tender but not brown.
3 Stir in the flour, cooking until frothy. Gradually add the vegetable stock, stirring continuously until the sauce thickens.
4 Add the sweetcorn and ricotta. Heat gently and season with basil, salt and pepper.
5 Serve lisci piping hot with sweetcorn and ricotta sauce poured over. Garnish with extra basil if wished.

Serves 4

pumpkin and sweet basil pasta

420 gram can **Wattie's Condensed Pumpkin Soup**
2 tblsp chopped fresh basil, or 1 tsp dried sweet basil
¼ cup white wine
¼ cup cream
4 cups dried spiral pasta
½ cup roasted pinenuts
4 rashers bacon, cooked until crispy
about ½ cup grated parmesan cheese
few basil sprigs (optional)

1 In a saucepan simmer together the soup with the basil and wine until hot. Stir in the cream and keep warm without boiling.
2 Cook the pasta in boiling, salted water until 'al dente'. Drain well.
3 Toss in the sauce.
4 Serve in large, wide bowls, garnished with the pinenuts, crumbled, crispy bacon rashers, parmesan cheese and basil if using.

Serves 4

tomato and olive pasta

1 tblsp minced garlic
2 x 400 gram cans **Wattie's Mediterranean Tomatoes**
¼ cup finely chopped black olives
2 tblsp finely chopped capers
50 gram can anchovies, drained and chopped
¼ cup olive oil
¼ cup white wine
salt and pepper to season
500 grams fettuccini or spaghetti
1–2 tblsp extra olive oil to toss the pasta with

1 In a saucepan put the garlic, tomatoes, olives, capers, anchovies, olive oil and white wine and bring to a simmer for 15 minutes until reduced by one third. Season with salt and pepper.
2 Cook the fettuccini or spaghetti in boiling, salted water until 'al dente'. Drain and toss in a little extra oil. Toss the pasta in the tomato and olive sauce and serve garnished with basil leaves, slices of parmesan cheese and a few whole olives or capers if wished.

Serves 4

smoked fish and pasta salad

2½ cups pasta spirals
1 tblsp oil (olive is nice here)
500 grams smoked fish
¼ cup chopped fresh parsley or dill
grated rind and juice 1 lemon
6 spring onions, trimmed and chopped
½ cup **Wattie's Tartare Sauce**
salt and pepper to season

1 Cook the pasta spirals in plenty of boiling, salted water for 12 minutes until 'al dente'. Drain well and cool in plenty of cold water. Drain well and toss with the oil.
2 Flake the flesh from the smoked fish.
3 In a bowl toss together the pasta, smoked fish, herbs, lemon rind and juice, spring onion and tartare sauce. Season with salt and pepper to serve.

Serves 4

pumpkin and sweet basil pasta

crispy sesame chicken and avocado on pasta

pasta
2 chicken breasts, with skin on
1 tblsp honey
1 tblsp sesame seeds
4 cups dried pasta shapes (your choice)
2–3 spring onions, trimmed
1–2 avocados, halved and stoned
100 grams mangetout or green beans
¼ cup roughly chopped, fresh parsley or coriander

ginger dressing
½ 300 gram bottle of **Wattie's Bit on the Side Sweet Chilli Sauce**
1 tblsp minced fresh ginger
1 tblsp honey
1 tblsp sesame oil (optional)
2 tblsp lemon or lime juice
salt and pepper to season

pasta
1. Spread the chicken with the honey and sprinkle over the sesame seeds. **(a)** Bake the chicken skin-side up on a foil-lined tray at 200°C for 25 minutes. Set aside to cool and then slice.
2. Cook the pasta in boiling, salted water until tender. **(b)** Drain and cool under running cold water. Drain.
3. Slice the spring onions, avocado and mangetout or green beans. **(c)**
4. In a bowl toss together the sliced chicken, pasta, spring onion, avocado, mangetout, parsley or coriander and Ginger Dressing. **(d)** Serve soon after making.

ginger dressing
1. In a jar shake together the sauce, ginger, honey, sesame oil if you have it, lemon or lime juice. Season with salt and pepper.

Serves 4

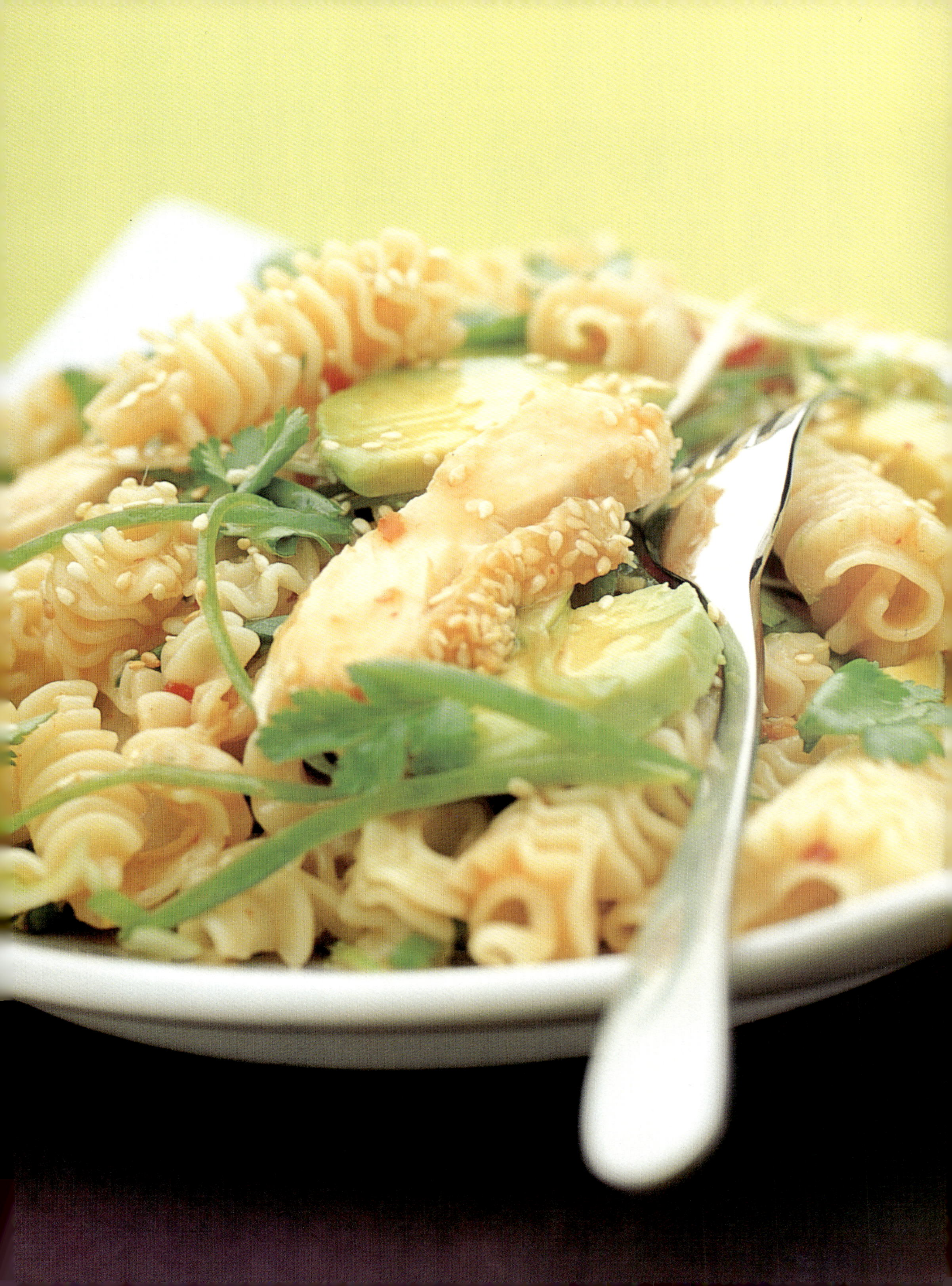

quick lemon and tuna risotto

1 onion, peeled and finely diced
1 tsp minced fresh garlic
2 tblsp oil
2 cups risotto or short-grain rice
4½ cups chicken stock
grated rind 1 lemon
1 tblsp chopped fresh oregano or marjoram
¼–½ cup finely grated parmesan cheese
150 gram pouch **Greenseas Lemon and Cracked Pepper Tuna**
parmesan cheese
black olives
sprigs oregano

1. Cook the onion and garlic in the oil in a large saucepan for 3–5 minutes until tender. Add the risotto or short-grain rice and stock and simmer over a low heat, stirring constantly for 30 minutes until the rice has absorbed all the stock, is tender and the risotto is creamy.

2. Stir in the lemon rind, oregano or marjoram and parmesan and, once the cheese has melted, flake in the tuna and stir gently to mix.

3. Serve in bowls garnished with parmesan cheese, black olives and oregano.

Serves **4**

chicken and spinach risotto

1 tblsp oil
1 onion, peeled and diced
4 chicken thigh fillets, finely diced
2 cups arborio rice
420 gram can **Wattie's Condensed Creamy Chicken Soup**
¼ cup dry white wine
3 cups chicken stock or water
2–3 cups well-packed, tender spinach leaves
½ cup finely grated parmesan cheese

1. Heat the oil in a large, lidded saucepan, add the onion and chicken and cook over a moderately high heat for 3–5 minutes, until the chicken is browned and the onion softened.

2. Add the rice and toss to coat in the onion.

3. Add the soup, wine and chicken stock or water and stir to mix well. Cover and simmer very gently for 25 minutes, stirring occasionally until the rice is tender and all the liquid has been absorbed.

4. Stir in the spinach and parmesan cheese and stand for 2 minutes, to allow the spinach to wilt and the parmesan to melt.

5. Serve in bowls garnished with shavings of parmesan cheese.

Serves **4**

paella

2 double **Tegel Chicken Breasts**, without skin
2–3 tblsp oil
1 onion, peeled and finely diced
2–3 tsp minced garlic
1 tsp each mild chilli, turmeric and cumin
1½ cups long-grain rice

400 gram can **Wattie's Italian Seasoned Tomatoes**
1 cup water or chicken stock
100 grams finely sliced salami or chorizo sausage
1 cup frozen **Wattie's Freshlock™ Baby Peas**
¼ cup dry sherry

1. Cut the chicken breasts into large pieces.
2. Heat the oil in a large frying pan, add the chicken pieces and brown quickly over a high heat. Once browned, add the onion, garlic, spices and rice. Cook for 1 minute.
3. Stir in the tomatoes, water or chicken stock and salami and stir to even out all the ingredients. Cover and lower to a gentle simmer for 20 minutes.
4. Sprinkle over peas, cover and stand for 5 minutes before fluffing up with a fork.
5. Pour over the sherry just before serving. Serve with a crisp salad.

Serves 4

spanish pasta salad

salad
4 cups pasta spirals or another favourite shape
½ cup **Wattie's Tomato Sauce**
2 tblsp wine vinegar (red is nice here)
¼ cup olive oil
1 tsp minced garlic
2 small green chillis, diced
¼ cup chopped mint
¼ cup chopped fresh basil
1 cup cherry tomatoes
salt and pepper to season
100 grams prosciutto

garnish
basil leaves
8–10 stuffed green olives

1. Cook the pasta in boiling, salted water for 10–12 minutes or until 'al dente'. Drain and cool.
2. In a large bowl mix the tomato sauce with the wine vinegar, olive oil, garlic, chilli, herbs and cherry tomatoes. Add the cold pasta and toss gently to mix. Season with salt and pepper.
3. Arrange the pasta on a serving platter with the prosciutto on top.
4. Garnish with basil leaves and chopped stuffed green olives.

Serves 4

thai tuna fritters

200 gram can **Greenseas Tuna Gourmet Thai Curry Style**
2 cups cooked rice
3 spring onions, finely sliced
1 tblsp chopped lemon grass*
2 tblsp chopped fresh coriander or parsley
1 tsp minced garlic
1 tsp minced red chilli
3 eggs
2 tblsp fish sauce
oil for pan-frying

1. In a large bowl mix together the tuna, rice, spring onion, lemon grass, coriander or parsley, garlic and red chilli.
2. Whisk together the eggs and fish sauce and add to the rice mixture. Mix well.
3. Heat sufficient oil to coat the bottom of the frying pan and when hot add large spoonfuls of the rice mixture. Cook for 2–3 minutes before flipping and cooking the other side.
4. Serve the tuna fritters with your favourite salad greens and accompanied with chilli sauce.

Makes 12 Serves 4–6

*Use fresh or bottled. If you do not have lemon grass use the grated rind of 2 lemons.

pasta pie

500 gram packet penne pasta
1 tblsp oil
1 onion, peeled and finely chopped
500 grams minced beef
1 tblsp minced garlic
400 gram can **Wattie's Italian Seasoned Tomatoes**
2 tblsp **Wattie's Tomato Paste**
1 cup chopped fresh basil or 2 tblsp dried
1 cup grated parmesan cheese
1 cup grated cheddar cheese

1. Cook the pasta in boiling, salted water until 'almost cooked'. Drain.
2. Heat the oil in a pan and brown the onion and mince for 5 minutes over a moderately high heat. Stir in the garlic and cook for a further minute. This is best done in two batches so the mince does not stew.
3. Add the tomatoes and tomato paste and cook for 2–3 minutes. Toss the mince mixture, pasta, basil and half the parmesan and cheddar cheeses.
4. Turn into a well-greased 6–8-cup-capacity ovenproof dish. Top with the remaining cheeses. Bake at 180°C for 25–30 minutes. Allow to cool before cutting into wedges. (This can be eaten hot or cold.)
5. Serve with your favourite salad on the side.

Serves 6

top right spanish pasta salad
middle left thai tuna fritters
bottom right pasta pie

cheese and rice croquettes

1 leek, white only, finely sliced
1 tblsp butter
1 cup short-grain rice
290 gram can **Wattie's Very Special Creamy Country Chicken Soup**
1–1½ cups chicken stock or water
100–150 grams blue cheese, crumbled
¼ cup pinenuts
salt and pepper to season
flour for dusting
butter or oil for pan-frying

to crumb

1 egg
¼ cup milk
2 cups dry breadcrumbs

1. Cook the leek in the butter in a saucepan for 5 minutes until tender. Stir in the rice and toss to coat in the butter.
2. Heat the soup in the microwave for 2 minutes. Remove and pour into the rice mix with the stock or water. Cook over a low heat for 20 minutes or until the rice is tender and has absorbed the liquid.
3. Allow to cool, then stir in the blue cheese and pinenuts. Season. Shape into small croquettes.
4. Mix together egg and milk. Dip the croquette into the egg and coat in the crumbs.
5. Pan-fry croquettes in a little oil for 5–6 minutes, turning regularly until golden.

Serves **4**

pasta with feta crumble

100 grams feta cheese, diced
2 spring onions, trimmed and finely chopped
1 yellow or red pepper, diced
2–3 tblsp chopped fresh basil or parsley
½ cup pinenuts, toasted
2 tblsp oil (olive is nice here)
pepper to season
200–250 grams dried pasta (your favourite shapes)
400 gram pouch **Wattie's Simply Cuisine Tuscan Pasta Sauce**

1. In a bowl toss together the feta cheese, spring onion, pepper, herbs, pinenuts and oil. Season with pepper and set aside for 10 minutes to marinate.
2. Cook the pasta in plenty of boiling, salted water until cooked. Strain and return to the saucepan.
3. Stir in the contents of the pasta sauce.
4. Serve the pasta in a shallow bowl, topped with the feta crumble.

Serves **2**

chicken and mushroom pilaf

500 grams **boneless** Tegel Chicken Thigh Fillets, without skin
2 tblsp oil
1 tblsp butter
1 onion, peeled and finely diced
2 tsp minced garlic
2 cups long-grain rice

4 cups chicken stock
1 bay leaf
½ tsp salt
250 grams flat field mushrooms, sliced
1 cup frozen **Wattie's Freshlock™ Baby Peas**
½ cup toasted cashew nuts to garnish

1. Cut the chicken into 2 cm pieces. Pan-fry in the hot oil in a flameproof pan in batches for 3–4 minutes until lightly cooked. Set aside.

2. Turn the heat down, add the butter to the pan with the onion and cook until tender for 1–2 minutes. Add the garlic and rice and cook for 1 minute or until the rice begins to whiten.

3. Pour in the stock and add the bay leaf, salt, sliced mushrooms and chicken. Bring to the boil, cover and transfer to a 175°C oven for 15 minutes.

4. Remove and stir the peas through. Cover and return to the oven for a further 5 minutes. Remove and stand for 5 minutes. Fluff with a fork and sprinkle with cashews to serve.

Serves 6

mushroom risotto

25 grams butter
1 onion, peeled and finely chopped
2 tsp minced garlic
2 cups short-grain rice
1 cup dry white wine
3½ cups chicken stock

420 gram can **Wattie's Condensed Creamy Mushroom Soup**
½ cup grated parmesan cheese
¼ cup cream
salt and pepper to season

1. Heat the butter in a large saucepan, add the onion and cook over a moderately low heat for 3–5 minutes until very soft but not coloured. Add the garlic and cook for a further minute.
2. Add the rice and cook for 1 minute until the rice begins to turn white.
3. Add the wine and stir constantly over a moderately low heat until the rice has absorbed all the wine. Add the chicken stock to the risotto, ½ cup at a time, stirring continuously. When each amount has been absorbed, add the next measure.
4. When all the stock has been added, stir in the mushroom soup and continue to cook over a low heat until the risotto is thick and creamy. Add the parmesan cheese and cream and season with salt and pepper.
5. Serve as is in bowls garnished with extra parmesan cheese, or on top of grilled mushrooms garnished with crispy bacon rashers, parmesan cheese and chopped parsley if wished.

Serves 4–6

chicken and turkey

{chicken and turkey}
tips and hints

1 Smoked chicken is cooked. It is ideal to tear into pieces and toss into pasta, salads or pies. It can be enjoyed hot or cold and is available whole or as boneless breasts.

2 A roast chicken can easily be carved into 8 pieces for serving. Cut down either side of the breast to remove the leg and thigh portions. Carefully pull away or cut the breast off from each side of the bird. This leaves only the carcass, which can be discarded. The portions can be served as is or you can cut them in half and serve each person with a little breast and thigh meat.

3 When glazing puff pastry for a pie (see Cranberry and Chicken Pie, page 82) brush the glaze just to the edge of the pastry. If you brush the edges of puff pastry with a glaze the layers of pastry will 'glue together' and not rise as well.

4 When browning chicken, make sure the oil is very hot so you can brown the chicken quickly. This will enhance both the flavour and the colour of the finished dish.

- If you are not sure what size chicken or how much to buy, here is a quick guide.

Whole Birds

Size 10 (1 kg)   Serves 3–4
Size 12 (1.2 kg) Serves 4
Size 14 (1.4 kg) Serves 5–6
Size 16 (1.6 kg) Serves 6
Size 18 (1.8 kg) Serves 6–7
Size 20 (2 kg)   Serves 7–8

Pieces

The weight of boneless chicken pieces, either breast or thigh portions, varies enormously, making it very difficult to give accurate cooking times. Allow 200 grams boneless chicken meat per person, or approximately 1 boneless breast or 3 boneless thigh portions without skin. Allow 1 leg and thigh joint per person. It may seem large, but there is a large percentage of waste from bone and skin.

Others

Allow 1 poussin per person.
Allow 2–3 drumsticks per person.

- Frozen chicken and turkey should always be defrosted in the refrigerator. When defrosting a whole turkey or chicken, always allow sufficient time. A turkey will take 3 days and chicken 1–2 days. Read instructions on the back of the packet.

- It is essential to store chicken correctly, both before and after cooking, to avoid any problems. Follow these rules always:

  - Refrigerate as soon as possible after purchase.
  - Store fresh chicken well wrapped in the coolest part of the refrigerator.
  - Use fresh chicken within 2–3 days after purchase.
  - Use chicken livers within 2 days after purchase.
  - Wipe your chopping board down thoroughly after cutting chicken and never cut anything on the board after cutting up raw chicken without washing it thoroughly. Bleach chopping boards regularly.

- If you are using dried herbs, place them in a sieve and run under cold water for a minute. It will help reconstitute the dried herbs. This is a great trick when herbs will not be cooked, as in a mayonnaise or salad.

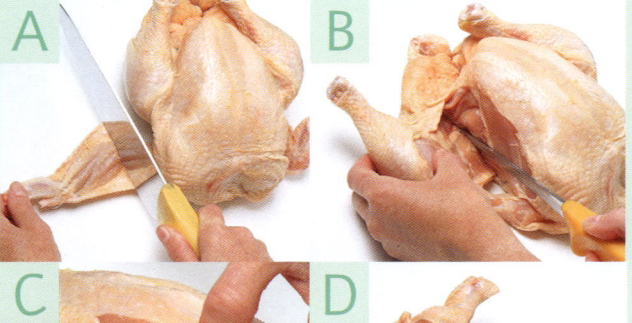

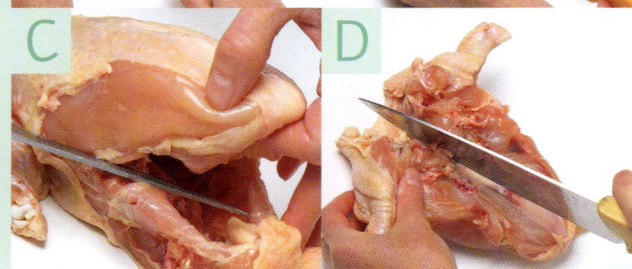

cutting up a chicken for casseroling

When making a casserole you can purchase chicken pieces or you can quickly cut a chicken into 8 even-sized pieces as follows:

A Cut off the wing tips at the second joint (use for stock).

B Using a sharp knife, cut down through the leg and thigh joint and pull it away from the body. Cut around the joint that attaches the thigh to the body. Cut between the leg and thigh joint to make the two pieces.

C Using a cook's knife or kitchen scissors, cut the breast horizontally away from the backbones. You will need to turn the bird over to cut the breast free.

D Cut the breast in half though the breast bone and then cut each breast diagonally in half again.

E You will have eight even-sized pieces, each with an equal amount of bone: perfect for a casserole.

honey chicken with avocado and orange salad

chicken
6 boneless Tegel Chicken Thigh Fillets (without skin)
1/2 cup **Good Taste Company Honey and Macadamia Nut Dressing**
grated rind and juice 1 orange
1 tblsp honey

avocado and orange salad
2 oranges
salad greens for 4
1/2 red onion, peeled and thinly sliced
2 avocados, halved, stoned, peeled and sliced
1/2 cup **Good Taste Company Honey and Macadamia Nut Dressing**
1/4 cup sour cream
few macadamia nuts, chopped for garnish

chicken
1. Place chicken portions in a dish. Pour over the dressing, orange rind and juice, honey and turn to coat. Cover and refrigerate for up to 4 hours.
2. Fan grill the chicken thighs at 200°C for 20 minutes until they are golden and cooked, or cook over a moderately hot barbecue, turning occasionally. Serve with the Avocado and Orange Salad.

avocado and orange salad
1. Grate the orange rind and place in a bowl. Cut away the thick, white pith and cut the flesh into thin slices. On a large platter, scatter the lettuce leaves, red onion, avocado and orange slices.
2. Mix the grated orange rind with the dressing and sour cream. Pour over the salad just before serving and garnish with the macadamia nuts if wished.

Serves 4

chicken pasta salad with sundried tomato dressing

200–250 grams cooked chicken or ham
1 red onion, peeled and finely chopped
1 red pepper, cored and finely chopped
1/4 cup finely chopped fresh basil
2 tblsp chopped fresh parsley
4–5 cups cooked pasta (spirals are nice here)
2 tblsp lemon juice
3/4 cup **Eta Creamy Sundried Tomato Dressing**
salt and pepper to season
2 tblsp chopped olives, optional
1 tblsp chopped capers, optional

1. Shred or cut the chicken or ham into small pieces and place in a bowl. Add the red onion, red pepper, basil, parsley, pasta, lemon juice and dressing. Season well with salt and pepper. If wished add the olives and capers.
2. Toss the salad together and serve soon after making.

Serves 4

Food in a Minute **THE COOKBOOK**

turkey plum stir-fry

500 grams **Tegel Fresh Turkey Breast**, finely sliced
425 gram can **Wattie's Stir Fry Spicy Plum Sauce**
2 tsp minced fresh garlic
2 tblsp oil

4 cups vegetables for stir-fry (use fresh or your favourite **Wattie's** frozen vegetables)
¼ cup cashew nuts to garnish

1. Toss the sliced turkey in half the can of plum sauce and garlic. Cover and leave for ½ hour.
2. Heat 1 tblsp oil in a wok and stir-fry vegetables, tossing quickly until tender. Set aside.
3. Heat the remaining oil in the wok. Stir-fry the turkey in two batches over a high heat until cooked.
4. Return the vegetables and remaining sauce to the wok and toss. Serve on rice, garnished with cashews.

Serves 4

easy chicken vegetable bake

2 large potatoes, peeled and finely sliced
500 grams boneless chicken thighs, diced
1 onion, peeled and finely diced
1 cup grated pumpkin or carrot
2–3 cups mixed fresh vegetables
420 gram can **Wattie's Condensed Creamy Chicken Soup**
2 tblsp chopped parsley
¼ cup each fresh breadcrumbs and grated cheese

1. Place the sliced potatoes in an overlapping layer in the base of a lasagne-style dish.
2. In a bowl, mix together the chicken, onion, grated pumpkin or carrot, vegetables, soup and parsley.
3. Spread the mixture evenly over the sliced potatoes. Sprinkle with the breadcrumbs and cheese.
4. Bake at 180°C for 40–45 minutes until golden and hot.

Serves **4**

creamy smoked chicken filo pie

2 medium red onions, peeled and sliced
1–2 tblsp oil
250 grams sliced button mushrooms
2 tblsp chopped marjoram or oregano
2 tblsp sliced sundried tomatoes (optional)
1 **Tegel Smoked Chicken**
250 gram tub **Tararua Crème Fraîche**
salt and pepper to season
12 sheets filo pastry
100 grams butter, melted

1. Cook the onion in the oil in a hot pan for 3 minutes. Add mushrooms and cook for a further 5 minutes. Add herbs and sundried tomatoes if using and cool.
2. Tear the smoked chicken into bite-sized pieces (discarding skin and bones). Toss into the mushroom mixture with the crème fraîche and season.
3. Brush 8 sheets of filo pastry with the melted butter and place in a 24 cm flan tin. Fill with the chicken and mushroom mixture and then flip the overhanging filo pastry edges into the centre. Brush the remaining sheets of filo with butter and place on top of the pie. Sprinkle with sesame seeds if wished and bake at 190°C for 40–45 minutes until golden and crispy.

Serves **6**

chicken jambalaya

2 tblsp oil
1 large onion, peeled and diced
2 stalks celery, finely diced
1 red or green pepper, diced
500 grams boneless Tegel Chicken Thigh Fillets, diced

1–2 spicy chorizo-style sausages, diced (optional)
400 gram can **Wattie's Cajun-Style Tomatoes**
1 cup long-grain rice
2 cups chicken stock
1 bay leaf (optional)

1. Heat the oil in a large, flameproof casserole and cook the onion, celery and pepper for 3–4 minutes until softened. Set aside.
2. Add the diced chicken and spicy sausage if using and brown quickly on all sides.
3. Return the vegetables to the pan with the tomatoes, rice, stock and bay leaf. Stir, cover and simmer gently for 15 minutes until the rice has absorbed almost all the liquid. (Alternatively, bake at 180°C for 20–25 minutes.)
4. Stand for 5 minutes before lifting the lid. Serve the jambalaya in shallow bowls, garnish with fresh thyme and have a salad on the side.

Serves 4

chicken cacciatore

1–2 tblsp oil
1 onion, peeled and sliced
1 tsp minced fresh garlic
250 grams button mushrooms, halved
6–8 boneless Tegel Chicken Thigh Fillets, without skin
½ cup white wine, water or chicken stock
420 gram can **Wattie's Condensed Big Red Tomato Soup**
sprig fresh thyme

1. Heat the oil in a lidded frying pan and quickly cook the onion, garlic and mushrooms for 2 minutes or until lightly brown. Set aside.
2. Add the chicken portions to the pan and brown quickly over a high heat.
3. Add the wine, water or chicken stock to the pan. Return the vegetables and add the soup and sprig of thyme.
4. Cover and simmer gently for 30 minutes or until the chicken is tender.
5. Serve on rice with your favourite green vegetables.

Serves 4

variation
- Add a rasher or two of chopped bacon if wished.

tuscan chicken

8 Tegel Chicken Drumsticks
1 tblsp flour
2 tblsp oil
2 onions, peeled and sliced
about 2 cups mushrooms, halved
400 gram can **Wattie's Italian Seasoned Tomatoes**
12 stuffed green olives
plenty of freshly ground black pepper
pasta for 4 to accompany (shape of your choice)

1. Remove the skin from the drumsticks if wished. Put the flour into a bag and toss the chicken legs in the flour.
2. Heat the oil in a large, lidded, non-stick frying pan. Add the chicken pieces and brown over a moderately high heat for 10 minutes, turning regularly so that the chicken browns evenly.
3. Add the onions, mushrooms, tomatoes and olives and season well with freshly ground black pepper.
4. Cover and simmer over a low heat for 25–30 minutes until the chicken drumsticks are cooked and tender.
5. Serve on pasta, garnished with fresh herbs if wished.

Serves 4

butter chicken

6 Tegel Chicken Leg and Thigh Portions, without skin
1 medium onion, peeled and quartered
1 cup natural, unsweetened yoghurt
1 tsp each ground ginger and garam masala
1/4 tsp chilli powder

2 x 400 gram cans **Wattie's Indian Spiced Tomatoes**
1/2 cup cream
an oversized knob of butter (about 50 grams)
2 tblsp chopped fresh coriander (optional)

1. Cut the chicken portions in half. Slash each portion through to the bone in three places. Place in one layer in a non-metallic dish.

2. In a food processor, process the onion, yoghurt and spices. Pour over the chicken and turn to coat evenly. Cover and refrigerate for at least 1 hour or up to 8 hours. (The longer you can leave the chicken to marinate, the more intense the flavour will be.)

3. Remove the chicken from the marinade and brush off any excess.

4. Bake at the top of the oven on a grill tray at 230°C for 20–25 minutes until well browned and cooked.

5. While the chicken is cooking, prepare the sauce. Simmer the two cans of tomatoes in a saucepan until reduced by half. Stir in the cream, butter and coriander, if used, and keep warm. Do not boil, or the sauce will curdle. Serve the chicken coated in the butter sauce.

6. Serve with rice, poppadums, chutneys and fresh bananas, sliced and tossed in lemon juice and desiccated coconut.

Serves 4–6

chicken with mustard crème fraîche sauce

2 tblsp oil or butter
4 Tegel Chicken Breasts
125 grams mushrooms, sliced (1 1/2 cups sliced)
1 onion, peeled and finely chopped
1 tblsp prepared mustard (French or Dijon is nice here)
250 gram tub Tararua Crème Fraîche
salt and pepper to season

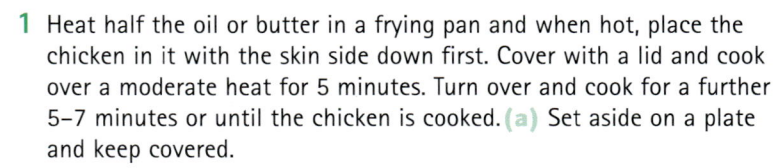

1. Heat half the oil or butter in a frying pan and when hot, place the chicken in it with the skin side down first. Cover with a lid and cook over a moderate heat for 5 minutes. Turn over and cook for a further 5–7 minutes or until the chicken is cooked. (a) Set aside on a plate and keep covered.

2. Add the remaining oil or butter to the pan and when hot, stir in the mushrooms and onion and cook over a moderate heat, stirring regularly until the vegetables are softened. (b)

3. Stir in the mustard and crème fraîche and bring to a gentle simmer. (c)

4. Return the chicken to the pan, cover and heat through for a further 3–4 minutes. (d) Season well with salt and pepper.

5. Serve with vegetables.

Serves 4

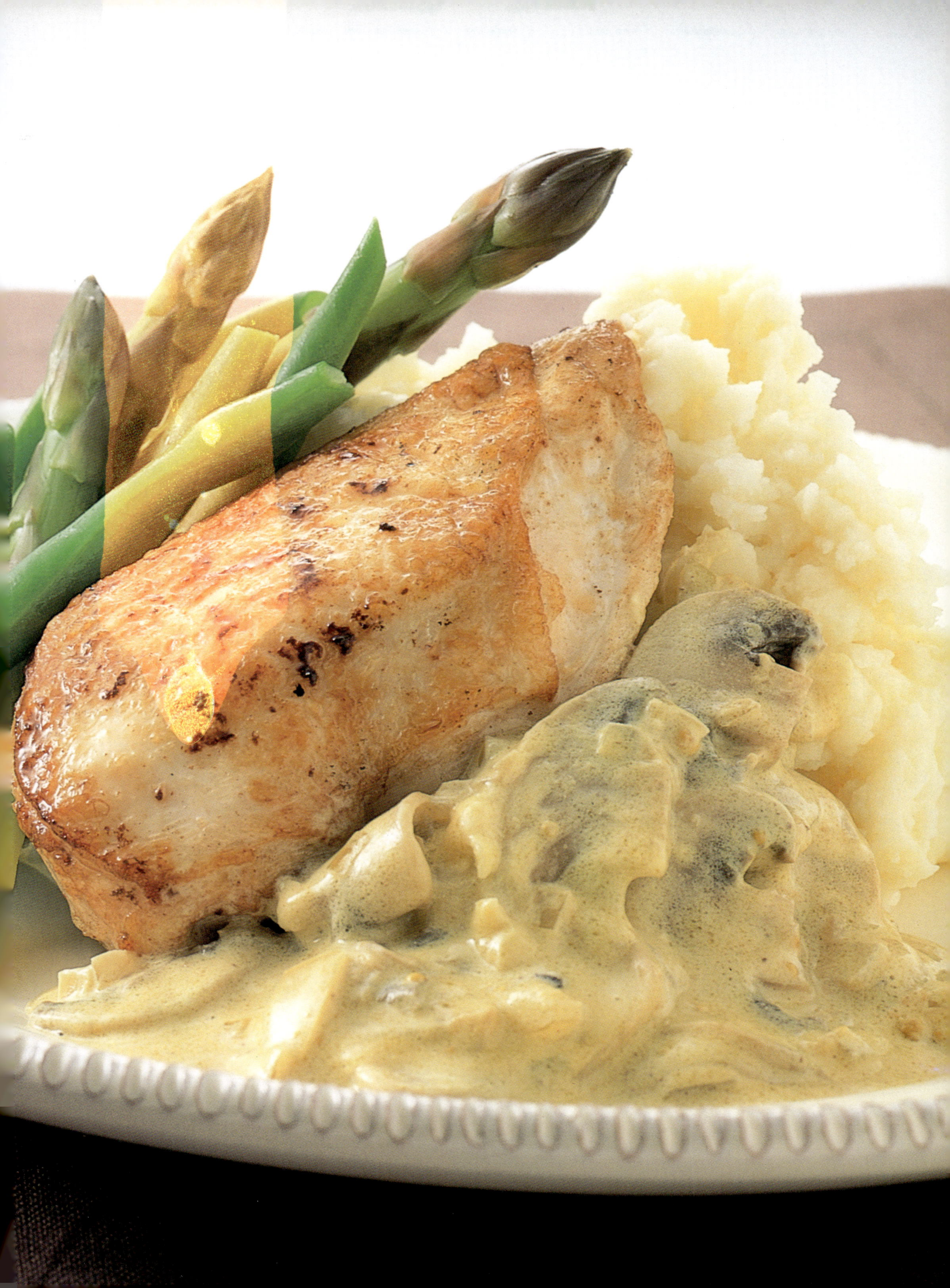

cranberry and chicken pie

1 double breast chicken, without skin
1 cup water
2 tblsp oil
1 onion, peeled and diced
2 tsp minced garlic
1–2 ham steaks, diced
½ cup **Wattie's Bit on the Side Cracker Cranberry Sauce**
2 tblsp sour cream
3 sheets pre-rolled puff pastry
milk or beaten egg to glaze

1. Poach chicken in the water in a lidded frying pan for 15 minutes or until cooked. Remove and cool.
2. Heat the oil in a frying pan and cook the onion and garlic until softened but not brown. Shred the chicken and put in a bowl with the onion mixture, ham, cranberry sauce and sour cream.
3. Place 1 puff pastry sheet on a greased baking tray. Pile the chicken and ham filling on top, leaving a 2 cm border around the outside. Brush with milk or beaten egg.
4. Roll the remaining 2 sheets of pastry together, large enough to cover the top. Fold in half, leaving a 3 cm border around all edges, cut 1 cm wide strips through the fold.
5. Open out and carefully place on top of the pie, pressing the edges together firmly. Trim the edges so they are even. Brush with milk or beaten egg to glaze.
6. Bake at 220°C for 30 minutes until the pastry is well risen and golden. Serve hot or cold in wedges.

Serves 6

chicken and asparagus bake

chicken
4 Tegel Chicken Leg and Thigh Portions
1½ cups chicken stock
1 onion, peeled and diced
2 tsp minced garlic
50 grams butter
4 tblsp flour
¼ cup cream
¼ cup chopped fresh parsley (or 1 tblsp dried)
340 gram can **Wattie's Asparagus Spears**, well drained
salt and pepper to season

crumble topping
25 grams butter
1½ cups fresh breadcrumbs
¼ cup grated cheddar or edam cheese

chicken

1. Cook the chicken portions in the stock for 35–40 minutes or until cooked. Remove, cool and reserve stock.
2. In a medium-sized saucepan cook the onion and garlic in the butter over a low-to-moderate heat for about 5–7 minutes until the onion has softened.
3. Add the flour and cook for 1 minute. Stir in the reserved chicken stock and keep stirring until the sauce thickens. Cook 2–3 minutes before stirring in the cream, parsley and asparagus. Season.
4. Pull the meat from the chicken bones and fold into the sauce. Spread into an ovenproof dish. Sprinkle over the crumble topping.
5. Bake at 190°C for 30 minutes until hot and golden.

crumble topping
1. Rub the butter into the crumbs and stir through the grated cheese.

Serves 4

crispy orange roast chicken with gravy

chicken
1 Whole Tegel Chicken
1 large orange, halved
few sprigs thyme
salt and pepper to season
1–2 tblsp butter, melted
1 tblsp flour

basic gravy
4 tblsp butter or fat from the roast chicken
4 tbsp flour
2 cups chicken stock
salt and pepper to season

chicken

1. Remove the chicken from the bag, remembering to note the weight of the chicken. Rinse well and pat dry.
2. Place the orange halves and thyme leaves inside the bird. Season with salt and pepper. Brush with the butter and sift over the flour.
3. Place on a roasting rack. Roast at 180°C for 30 minutes per 500 grams or until cooked. To check if the bird is cooked, pierce the chicken between the leg and thigh joints. If the juice is clear the bird is cooked. If the juice is pink, return the chicken to the oven for a further 10 minutes.
4. Remove the chicken from the roasting dish and allow to stand for 10 minutes to rest (and while you make the gravy).

basic gravy

1. If wished, drain off the fat from the roasting pan and reserve 4 tablespoons. Leave all the sediment in the pan as this adds flavour to your gravy.
2. Heat the fat or butter in the roasting dish. Add the flour and cook over a moderate heat for 1 minute or until frothy.
3. To avoid any lumps forming, gradually stir in the stock and simmer for 5 minutes, stirring occasionally. Season with salt and pepper.

Serves 4–6 (depending on size of chicken)

chicken laksa

1 tblsp oil
350–500 grams Tegel Chicken Breast, without skin, finely sliced
1 tsp each minced fresh ginger, garlic and chilli
2 tsp ground coriander
2 packets **Wattie's Spicy Chicken 99% Fat Free Noodles**
3 cups water
400 ml can lite coconut cream
100 grams snowpeas or green beans, finely sliced
2–3 spring onions, trimmed and finely chopped
1–2 tblsp Asian fish sauce (optional)
salt and pepper to season
chopped fresh coriander to garnish

1. Heat the oil in a large frying pan or wok and cook the chicken over a moderate heat until golden. Set aside. Add the ginger, garlic, chilli and coriander and cook for 1 minute.
2. Add the noodles and flavour sachet with the water, coconut cream, snowpeas or beans, spring onion and fish sauce. Season with salt and pepper and simmer for 1 minute. Return the chicken and simmer gently for about 3–4 minutes until the noodles are tender.
3. Serve garnished with coriander.

Serves **4**

farmhouse roast chicken with roasted baby beetroot

1.5 kg Whole Tegel Chicken
1 orange, quartered
6–8 large garlic cloves
2 tblsp fresh rosemary leaves or 1 tsp dried rosemary
salt and pepper to season
820 gram can **Wattie's Whole Baby Beetroot**, drained
2 tblsp honey

1. Wash the chicken and pat dry inside and out. Push the orange quarters, garlic and rosemary into the chicken cavity and tie the legs together. Place in a roasting dish and season with salt and pepper.
2. Roast at 180°C for 1 hour. Arrange the beetroot around the sides of the chicken. Cook a further 30 minutes.
3. Transfer the chicken to a serving platter. Pour the honey on top of the beetroot and toss over a moderate heat for about 1 minute. Arrange on the platter with the chicken. Accompany with gravy if wished. (See Crispy Orange Roast Chicken, page 83.)

Serves **6**

hunter-style chicken on rice

chicken
8 Tegel Chicken Drumsticks
1/4 cup seasoned flour
2–3 tblsp oil
2 onions, peeled and sliced
250 grams mushrooms, quartered
420 gram can **Wattie's Garlic Pasta Sauce**
2 tblsp chopped fresh rosemary
4 big garlic cloves, crushed, peeled and sliced (optional)

rice
2 tblsp oil
1 onion, peeled and finely chopped
2 cups long-grain rice
3 cups hot water or chicken stock
1 tsp salt

chicken

1 Remove the skin from the chicken and toss the chicken in the seasoned flour.

2 Heat the oil in a lidded frying pan. Add the chicken and brown well.

3 Add the onion, mushrooms, pasta sauce, rosemary and garlic if using.

4 Cover and simmer gently for 30 minutes.

rice

1 Heat the oil in a saucepan. Add the onion and cook over a low heat for 5–8 minutes until soft. Add the rice and toss to coat in the oil.

2 Add the hot water or stock and salt. Stir, cover, lower the heat to the lowest setting and simmer gently for 12 minutes until tender. Stand for 5 minutes before fluffing with a fork.

Serves 4

peach and roast turkey salad

salad
1 Rolled, Frozen Tegel Turkey Breast, defrosted
1 bunch asparagus or 200 grams snowpeas
410 gram can **Wattie's Peach Slices in Clear Juice**, well drained or 2–3 fresh peaches, sliced
2–3 spring onions, trimmed and finely chopped
handful of your favourite sprouts (optional)
lettuce for 6

dressing
1 cup **Eta Mayo Tangy American Style Mayonnaise**
grated rind and juice 1 orange
½ cup plain unsweetened yoghurt

salad
1 Cook the turkey roll according to the directions on the packet. Cool, then cut the breast into slices.
2 Blanch the asparagus or snowpeas in boiling, salted water for 2 minutes. Refresh in cold water and drain well.
3 In a large bowl toss together the turkey, asparagus or snowpeas, peaches, spring onions, sprouts and lettuce leaves. Arrange on a serving platter and pour the dressing over just before serving.

dressing
1 Blend together the mayonnaise with the orange rind and juice and yoghurt.

Serves **6**

warm chicken, grape and herb salad

1.5 kg Whole Tegel Chicken
½ lemon

dressing and salad
1 tblsp oil
2 tblsp white wine vinegar
2 tblsp liquid honey
grated rind and juice 1 lemon
2–3 tblsp chopped fresh herbs
300 grams your favourite pasta shape
2–3 spring onions, sliced
100 grams green grapes, halved if large
3 sticks celery, thinly sliced

1 Wash the chicken, pat dry with absorbent paper, rub with half a cut lemon, inside and out. Roast at 180°C for about 1½ hours, or until cooked.
2 Prepare the dressing by mixing the oil, vinegar, honey, lemon rind and juice with freshly chopped herbs.
3 About 10 minutes before the chicken is cooked, cook the pasta in boiling, salted water until 'al dente'. Drain well.
4 Cut hot, cooked chicken into bite-sized pieces and toss with warm pasta, spring onion, grapes, celery and dressing. Serve immediately.

Serves **5–6**

smoked chicken and melon salad

1 Tegel Smoked Chicken or 2 Tegel Smoked Chicken Breast Fillets
½ cantaloupe (rock melon)
½ honeydew melon
2–3 tomatoes
½–¾ cup **Eta Creamy Pesto Dressing**
¼ cup chopped fresh parsley or basil leaves

1 Pull the meat from the whole chicken. Cut or pull the smoked chicken meat into bite-sized pieces. If using chicken breast fillets, cut into bite-sized pieces.
2 Scoop the seeds from the melons and cut away the skin. Dice or slice the melons into 2 cm pieces.
3 Cut the tomatoes into thin wedges.
4 Toss the smoked chicken, melon, tomatoes and pesto dressing together and arrange on a serving plate. Sprinkle over the parsley or basil.

Serves **4–6**

top left peach and roast turkey salad

middle right smoked chicken and melon salad

bottom left warm chicken, grape and herb salad

chicken in a pot

4 tblsp oil
1 onion, peeled and chopped
2 stalks celery, trimmed and chopped
500 gram bag frozen **Wattie's Freshlock™ Baby Carrots**
6–8 pieces boneless **Tegel Chicken Fillets**
400 gram can **Wattie's Tomatoes and Courgettes**
2 potatoes, well scrubbed, not peeled

1. Heat half the oil in a large frying pan and quickly brown the onion and celery. Transfer to a large casserole and sprinkle the frozen carrots over the vegetables.
2. Return the frying pan to the heat and add the remaining oil. Quickly brown the chicken pieces over a high heat.
3. Arrange the chicken pieces on top of the vegetables. Pour over the tomatoes and courgettes and spread out evenly.
4. Cut the potatoes into thin slices and arrange evenly, overlapping each other, over the top.
5. Cover and cook at 180°C for 1¼ – 1½ hours until the potatoes are tender and the chicken is cooked.

Serves 4–6

moroccan chicken and apricot stew

8 **Tegel Chicken Drumsticks**
dash oil
2 onions, peeled and finely chopped
1 cup finely sliced dried apricots
1 tsp ground ginger
1 tsp ground coriander
1 cup chicken stock
400 gram can **Wattie's Mediterranean Tomatoes**
few black olives (optional)
chopped parsley or coriander

1. Brown the chicken in the oil over a moderate heat in a large, lidded frying pan until golden on all sides.
2. Add the onion, sliced apricots, ginger, coriander, stock and tomatoes and bring to the boil.
3. Cover and simmer gently for 30 minutes until the chicken drumsticks are cooked.
4. Serve with black olives, chopped parsley or coriander if wished.

Serves 4

chicken and apricot casserole

4 Tegel Chicken Leg and Thigh Portions (skin removed if wished)
2 tblsp butter or oil
2 onions, peeled and chopped
2–4 rashers bacon, chopped (optional)
1 tblsp minced garlic

32 gram packet onion soup
1 cup apricot and orange juice or nectar
410 gram can **Wattie's Apricot Halves in Clear Juice**, well drained
salt and pepper to season

1. Cut the leg and thigh portions in half. Heat the butter or oil in a large, heatproof casserole and quickly brown the chicken pieces on all sides. Set the chicken aside.
2. Add the onion and bacon to the casserole and cook until softened and lightly browned. Add the garlic and cook for a further 2 minutes. Return the chicken to the casserole.
3. Mix the onion soup, apricot and orange juice or nectar together. Cover and add to the casserole with the apricots and bring to the boil.
4. Lower the heat, cover and simmer gently on top of the stove for 45–50 minutes or until tender. Alternatively, cook in an oven at 180°C for 1 hour. Season well with salt and pepper before serving with your favourite vegetables.

Serves 4

roast cranberry turkey

4.5 kg Frozen Tegel Turkey, defrosted
2 tblsp butter or oil
1 onion, peeled and diced
2 tsp minced fresh garlic
4 rashers bacon, diced
2 cups fresh white breadcrumbs or cooked rice
grated rind 2 oranges
½ cup raisins or Craisins
300 gram bottle **Wattie's Bit on the Side Cracker Cranberry Sauce**
salt and pepper to season
50 grams softened or melted butter
2 tblsp honey

1 Wash the turkey and pat dry using paper towels.

2 Heat the butter or oil in a frying pan and cook the onion, garlic and bacon until softened. Add the breadcrumbs, orange rind, raisins or Craisins, and ½ cup cranberry sauce and mix together. Season well with salt and pepper.

3 Fill the turkey cavity with the stuffing. Tie the turkey legs together and twist the wings under the body. Spread the butter on top of the turkey and place in a roasting dish.

4 Cook according to the times on the back of the Tegel packet.

5 Mix the remaining cranberry sauce with the honey and during the last 20 minutes of cooking time, brush the turkey regularly to glaze.

6 Serve the turkey hot with your favourite trimmings and vegetables or salads. Accompany with turkey gravy if wished. (Follow the instructions for Basic Gravy in Crispy Orange Roast Chicken, page 83.)

Serves 8–10

beef and lamb

{beef and lamb} tips and hints

1 Fresh meat will keep for 2–3 days in the refrigerator, while mince should be used within 2 days of purchase. Store raw meats on a plate, covered with plastic wrap and in the coolest part of the refrigerator. If defrosting meat in the fridge, sit it on a plate or in a dish. Raw meat must always sit under cooked meats and food in the fridge, to prevent any moisture dripping onto cooked foods.

2 Season steaks by rubbing well with salt, pepper and oil just before cooking. Do not salt meat too far in advance of cooking as it will draw the moisture out of the meat, making it tough and dry.

3 When browning meat for a casserole, quickly sear the cut pieces in a hot pan in a dash of oil. Browning the meat will add colour and flavour.

4 When browning mince, use the back of a spoon to break the mince up into small even-sized pieces. Brown in a hot pan in small batches. Do not allow the meat to stew in a lukewarm pan. If this happens, remove the mince, strain, reheat the pan and begin again.

5 Garlic has a much higher sugar content than onions, so add garlic to onions or meat once browned, to prevent it from burning before other ingredients are softened or browned. Burned garlic is bitter.

6 Cuts of beef that are great for casseroles include chuck steak, blade steak (a), shin steak (b), thick skirt steak, topside (c) and oxtail (d).

7 Lamb cuts for casseroles include forequarter (boned and diced) (e), round neck chops (f), shoulder and forequarter chops (g) and lamb shanks (h). When buying beef and lamb, look for the Quality Mark logo. It is a registered trademark of the New Zealand Beef and Lamb Marketing Board — your guarantee of quality lean New Zealand meat.

8 To add a richer flavour to casseroles, once the onions/vegetables and meat have been browned add tomato paste to the pan and cook, stirring, over a moderate heat until the tomato paste changes colour from bright red to brown/red. Add the remaining ingredients. Cooking the tomato paste concentrates flavour and caramelises the sugars, adding a rich flavour to casseroles.

9 Simmer casseroles, both beef and lamb, at 140–160°C to ensure the meat remains juicy and tender. Meat boiled rapidly at high temperatures, say 180–200°C, will be dry and tough, even though it is cooked in liquid.

10 When cooking meat, always allow resting time out of the hot pan, once cooked. This ensures the meat will be tender and juicy when carved. As a rule of thumb allow 5 minutes per 500 grams. For racks of lamb and steak, allow a good 3–5 minutes before carving.

glazed meatloaf

½ cup cooked barley or rice (brown rice is great)
500 grams **Quality Mark Lean Minced Beef**
2 tblsp chopped fresh oregano, or use 1 tsp dried
2 tblsp chopped fresh parsley
2 tblsp chopped fresh thyme, or use 1 tsp dried thyme
¼ cup **Wattie's Tomato Sauce**
2 spring onions, finely chopped
2 tsp minced garlic
1 egg
salt and pepper to season

glaze
2 tblsp each oil, honey, **Wattie's Tomato Sauce** and soy sauce

1. In a bowl mix together the cooked barley or rice, mince, oregano, parsley, thyme, tomato sauce, spring onion, garlic and egg. Season well with salt and pepper.
2. Shape into a loaf and set in an ovenproof dish, like a lasagne dish.
3. Mix the oil, honey, tomato sauce and soy sauce together and brush the glaze over the top.
4. Bake at 180°C for 60 minutes. Stand for 10 minutes before carving.
5. Serve with your favourite vegetables and sauce to accompany.

Serves 6

meatballs in madras curry

½ cup red lentils
1 onion, peeled and finely diced
500 grams **Quality Mark Lean Minced Beef**
1 egg
1 tsp each ground coriander, cumin and garam masala*
2 tblsp oil
415 gram can **Wattie's Madras Curry Sauce**
3 large tomatoes, finely chopped
¼ cup chopped fresh coriander or parsley

garnish
plain, unsweetened yoghurt and fresh coriander leaves

1. Soak the lentils in 1 cup water for 30 minutes. Drain.
2. In a bowl mix together the lentils, onion, mince, egg, coriander, cumin, garam masala or curry powder, salt and pepper. Shape into 12 even-sized meatballs.
3. Heat the oil in a lidded frying pan and brown the meatballs on all sides over a moderate heat.
4. Add the curry sauce and tomatoes and stir. Cover and simmer gently for 30 minutes until the meatballs are cooked. Stir in the chopped coriander or parsley.
5. Serve with rice, yoghurt and coriander.

Serves 4

Instead of the spices, use 1 tblsp curry powder and 1 tsp each of salt and pepper.

basic spaghetti sauce

2 tblsp olive oil
2 medium onions, finely chopped
2 rashers bacon, chopped
1 tblsp minced garlic
500 grams minced beef
1/2 cup tomato paste

2 x 400 gram cans **Wattie's Tomatoes in Juice**
1/2 cup beef stock
1 bouquet garni
1 sprig rosemary
salt and pepper to season
1/4 cup chopped fresh oregano

1. Heat the oil in a frying pan, add the onion and bacon and cook, tossing regularly, until the onion is golden. Add the garlic and cook for a further 2 minutes.

2. Remove the vegetables from the pan, set aside and add the meat to the hot pan. Break the meat up with a fork or spoon as you cook over a high heat to brown. Strain off any meat juices.

3. Return the onion mix to the pan and add the tomato paste, tomatoes and juice, stock, bouquet garni and rosemary and season well with salt and pepper. Cook over a low heat for 30 minutes, stirring regularly. Add the oregano just before serving over the spaghetti.

Makes 4 cups

Beef and Lamb

winter sausage pie

6 thick beef or pork sausages
1 tblsp oil
1 onion, peeled and diced
1 carrot, peeled and finely diced
1 parsnip, peeled and finely diced
1 stalk celery, diced
550 gram can **Wattie's Just Add Devilled Sausages Simmer Sauce**
3/4 cup water
500 gram packet **Wattie's Potato Pom Poms**
1/2 cup grated cheese, optional

1. Cook the sausages in a hot pan in the oil until well browned but only half cooked. Cool and slice thickly. Place in a large, lasagne-style dish.
2. Add the onion, carrot, parsnip and celery to the pan and cook for 5–6 minutes until lightly brown.
3. Pour in the simmer sauce and water, bring to the boil and simmer for 5 minutes. Carefully pour over the vegetables.
4. Arrange the pom poms on top and scatter over the cheese.
5. Bake at 190°C for 30 minutes.

Serves **4**

chilli con carne

dash oil
500 grams Quality Mark Lean Minced Beef
2 onions, peeled and sliced
1 tblsp minced garlic
1–3 tsp ground cumin (optional)
420 gram can **Wattie's Chilli Beans**
1/4 cup **Wattie's Tomato Sauce or Paste**
1 cup beef stock or water

1. Heat the oil in a lidded frying pan and brown the mince well, breaking it up with a fork or the back of a wooden spoon as you go. This may be best done in two batches. Set aside.
2. Add the onion, garlic and cumin to the pan and cook for 2–3 minutes until fragrant and the onion is just beginning to soften.
3. Return the minced meat to the pan with the chilli beans, tomato sauce or paste and beef stock or water.
4. Cover and simmer for 15 minutes until the beef is tender.
5. Serve on rice with crusty bread and a salad or your favourite winter vegetables.

Serves **4**

fruity devilled sausages

1 tblsp oil
8 really tasty, thick beef or pork sausages
1 apple, cored and thinly sliced
1 onion, peeled and sliced

½ cup sultanas
227 gram can pineapple pieces and juice
550 gram can **Wattie's Just Add Devilled Sausages Simmer Sauce**

1 Heat the oil in a frying pan and when hot add the sausages. Brown on all sides over a moderately low heat so they do not split their skins.

2 Add the apple, onion, sultanas, pineapple and juice and the simmer sauce.

3 Stir, cover and simmer over a low heat for 30 minutes.

4 Serve the sausages with plenty of hearty mashed potato and vegetables.

Serves 4

french beef and mushroom cottage pie

1 tblsp oil
1 onion, finely chopped
500 grams Quality Mark Lean Minced Beef
¼ cup tomato paste
545 gram can **Wattie's Just Add Country French Mince Simmer Sauce**
2 cups chopped mushrooms
1 cup leftover or frozen vegetables
1 cup water or beef stock
500 gram packet **Wattie's Potato Pom Poms**
½ cup grated tasty cheddar cheese

1. Heat the oil in a frying pan and brown the onion and minced beef, breaking up the beef with a spoon as you go to ensure even-sized pieces.
2. Add the tomato paste and cook, stirring over a moderate heat until it has darkened to a deep brown colour. This takes about 5 minutes and adds a wonderful rich flavour to the pie.
3. Add the simmer sauce, mushrooms, vegetables, and water or beef stock. Stir, cover and simmer for 15 minutes.
4. Transfer to a 6-cup-capacity ovenproof dish, top with pom poms and sprinkle over the grated cheese.
5. Bake at 220°C for about 15–20 minutes until the topping is golden, the cheese bubbling and the pie hot and delicious.

Serves 4–5

winter beef casserole

750 grams Quality Mark Cross-cut Beef (or other stewing beef)
2 tblsp seasoned flour
2–3 tblsp oil
½ cup **Wattie's Tomato Sauce**
2 tblsp **Lea & Perrins Worcestershire Sauce**
1½ cups beef stock
2 onions, peeled and roughly cut
2 stalks celery, trimmed and chopped
1 carrot, peeled and diced
250 grams mushrooms, halved
salt and pepper to serve
chopped parsley to garnish

1. Trim the meat of any extra fat and cut into large, 3 cm pieces. Toss the meat in the seasoned flour.
2. Heat the oil in a frying pan and when hot cook the meat over a high heat until it is well browned on all sides. Transfer to a casserole. Blend together the remaining seasoned flour with the tomato sauce, Worcestershire sauce and beef stock. Pour into the pan and bring to the boil. Transfer to the casserole.
3. Add the onion, celery, carrot and mushrooms. Cover.
4. Bake at 160°C for 1¼–1½ hours. Alternatively, simmer over a very low heat on top of the stove for the same amount of time. Stir occasionally. Season and sprinkle with chopped parsley before serving.

Serves 4

hearty beef and beer casserole

650–750 grams Quality Mark Blade or Chuck Steak
¼ cup seasoned flour
2 tblsp oil
355 ml can dark beer or Guinness
1 onion, peeled and roughly chopped
1 large carrot, peeled and roughly chopped
2 stalks celery, trimmed and chopped
1 large parsnip, peeled and roughly chopped
535 gram can **Wattie's Very Special Hearty Minestrone Soup**

1. Cut the meat into large, 3 cm pieces and toss in the seasoned flour.
2. Heat the oil in a large, lidded frying pan and brown the meat pieces on all sides. (Browning will add colour and flavour to the finished casserole.)
3. Add the beer and simmer, uncovered, for 5 minutes. You need to reduce the beer by a quarter.
4. Add the onion, carrot, celery, parsnip and soup and bring to a simmer. Cover and simmer gently for 1¼ hours until tender. Alternatively, transfer to a casserole and cook at 160°C for the same length of time.
5. Serve with mashed potatoes and vegetables.

Serves 4–6

variation
- If wished, add 250 grams button mushrooms and/or 4 rashers diced bacon.

top winter beef casserole
bottom french beef and mushroom cottage pie

country beef casserole

750 grams Quality Mark Cross-cut Blade Steak or other
    stewing steak (see Tips and Hints, page 93)
dash oil
1 leek, trimmed and washed
2 carrots, peeled and sliced
545 gram can **Wattie's Just Add Country French
    Mince Simmer Sauce**
about 12–16 mushrooms
1 cup frozen **Wattie's Freshlock™ Minted Baby Peas**
about 12 slices French bread
butter for spreading
1 cup grated cheddar cheese

1 Cut the beef into 3 cm pieces. Heat the oil in a frying pan and brown the meat over a high heat. (a) Transfer to a 3-litre-capacity casserole.

2 Cut the leek into long, finger-sized pieces and add to the casserole with the carrots, mushrooms and mince sauce. (b)

3 Cook at 160°C for 1¼ hours or until the meat is tender.

4 Stir through the peas. Spread the French bread slices with butter and place in an overlapping layer around the outside. (c)

5 Sprinkle the cheese over the bread slices. (d) Fan grill for about 8–10 minutes until the bread slices are golden.

6 Serve with mashed potatoes.

Serves 4–6

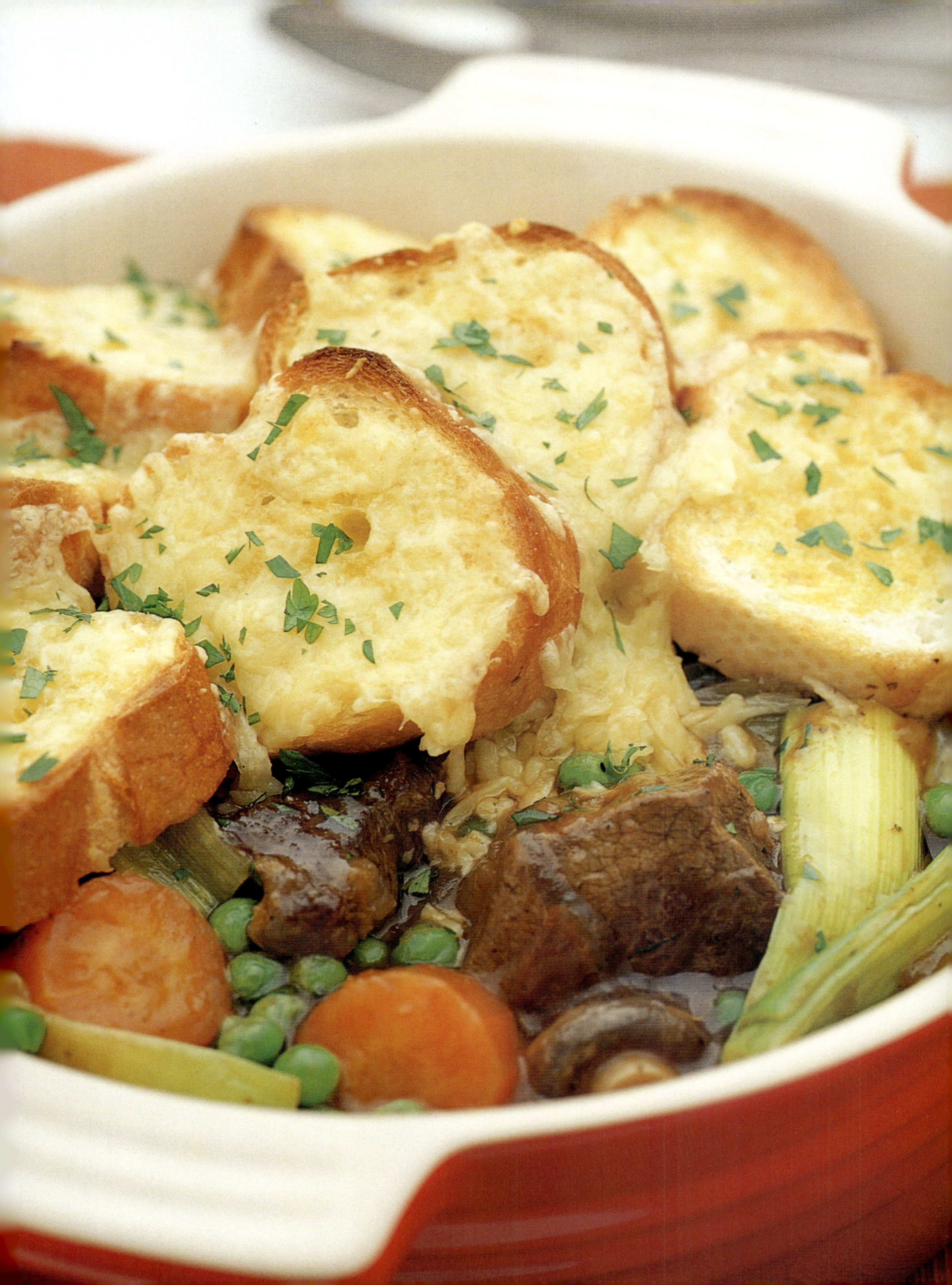

mexican beef and bean casserole

500 grams Quality Mark Chuck or Cross-cut Blade Steak
dash oil
2 onions, peeled and cut into 2 cm dice
1 tblsp paprika
400 gram can **Wattie's Whole Peeled Tomatoes in Purée**
425 gram can **Craig's Spicy Mexican Beans**
about 12 mushrooms, diced
½ cup beef stock or water

1. Cut the beef into large, 3 cm pieces. Heat the oil in a frying pan and brown the meat in two batches over a high heat and then transfer to a casserole.

2. Add the onion to the pan and cook for 2–3 minutes. Sprinkle over the paprika and cook for ½ minute before stirring in the tomatoes, beans, mushrooms and beef stock or water.

3. Bring to the boil and then pour over the beef. Cover and cook at 160°C for 1¼ hours until the meat is tender.

4. Serve hot with your favourite green vegetable.

Serves 4

herbed porcupines

500 grams Quality Mark Lean Minced Beef
½ cup uncooked, long-grain rice
¼ cup chopped fresh herbs, like thyme or parsley
salt and pepper to season
1 tblsp oil

1 onion, peeled and finely sliced
2 carrots, peeled and finely chopped
550 gram can **Wattie's Just Add Hearty Savoury Mince Simmer Sauce**
2 cups water

1. In a bowl mix together the minced beef, rice and herbs and season with salt and pepper.
2. Roll into 12–14 even-shaped balls.
3. Heat the oil in a frying pan and add the onion and carrot. Cook for 3–4 minutes until just softened. Add the simmer sauce and water and bring to the boil.
4. Add the meatballs and cover. Simmer gently for 30 minutes, turning once during the cooking time. Serve garnished with a little chopped fresh herb and your favourite seasonal vegetables.

Serves **4–6**

cheese burgers with sweet potato and orange salad

cheese burgers
750 grams Quality Mark Lean Minced Beef
1 cup grated or finely diced colby or edam cheese
½ cup chopped fresh parsley
1 small onion, finely diced
1 egg
2–3 slices bread, crumbed
½ cup **Wattie's Tomato** or **Barbecue Sauce**
salt and pepper to season

sweet potato and orange salad
1 kg kumara, peeled
2 large oranges
4 spring onions, trimmed and finely chopped
½ cup **Eta Potato Salad Dressing**
1 tsp curry powder

cheese burgers
1 Mix the lean minced beef, cheese, parsley, onion, egg, breadcrumbs and tomato sauce together.
2 Mould into 8 even-shaped patties and cook over a moderate heat on a greased barbecue or in a frying pan, for 5–7 minutes each side until the burgers are golden. Alternatively, you can grill the burgers under a moderately hot heat for the same time until cooked and golden.
3 Serve the burgers on a crispy bun, with salad topping and accompanied with Sweet Potato and Orange Salad.

sweet potato and orange salad
1 Cook the kumara in boiling salted water until just cooked. Drain and cool. Cut into slices or thick chunks.
2 Grate the rind from the oranges then cut away the bitter, white pith. Segment the oranges.
3 In a bowl mix together the kumara, orange rind and flesh, spring onion, salad dressing and the curry powder. Mix gently.
4 Serve in a salad bowl garnished with a little chopped fresh herbs, such as chives.

Serves 8

basic barbecue burgers

750 grams Quality Mark Lean Minced Beef
1 egg
3–4 spring onions, trimmed and finely chopped
¼ cup chopped fresh parsley or 2 tblsp dried parsley
about 4 large gherkins, finely chopped
¾ cup fresh wholemeal breadcrumbs
½ cup **Wattie's Tomato** or **Barbecue Sauce**
½ tsp each salt and pepper to season
1–2 tblsp oil (for pan-frying or barbecue)

1 In a bowl combine the minced beef, egg, spring onion, parsley, gherkins, breadcrumbs and barbecue sauce and season with salt and pepper. Mix well.
2 Mould into 8 patties with a wet hands.
3 Barbecue or grill for about 5–7 minutes on each side until the burgers are well browned and cooked. Serve in buns with your favourite toppings.

Serves 6–8

thai-scented burgers

500 grams Quality Mark Lean Minced Beef
2 tblsp chopped lemon grass
1 tblsp grated fresh ginger
3 cloves garlic, crushed, peeled and chopped
2 tsp ground coriander
1 tsp each salt and pepper
2 tblsp each chopped fresh mint and coriander or parsley
2 spring onions, trimmed and chopped
1 cup fresh breadcrumbs
1 egg
½ cup **Wattie's Bit on the Side Sweet Chilli Sauce**

1 In a bowl put the all ingredients and mix well. If you can, allow the mixture to stand for about 30 minutes.
2 Mould into 6 even-shaped burgers.
3 Barbecue, pan-fry or grill the burgers over a moderate heat, for 5–7 minutes each side, turning only once. Serve in a bun, with your favourite toppings.

Serves 4–6

cheese burger with
sweet potato and orange salad

thai beef salad with chilli lime dressing

salad
400 grams beef Scotch fillet, fillet or rump steak
2 tblsp each chopped fresh basil, coriander and mint
2 tsp each minced garlic and chilli
2 tblsp olive oil
2 carrots, peeled and finely sliced
100 grams snowpeas, sliced
150 grams cellophane rice noodles
4 spring onions, trimmed and shredded
½ telegraph cucumber, deseeded and sliced
mint leaves for garnish

dressing
½ cup **Wattie's Bit on the Side Sweet Chilli Sauce**
2 tsp minced fresh ginger
grated rind and juice 1 lime or lemon
¼ cup water

salad

1 Cut the beef into thin strips and place in a bowl with the basil, coriander, mint, garlic, chilli and oil. Toss to coat and allow to marinate for 20 minutes.

2 Blanch the carrot strips and snowpeas. Soak the cellophane noodles in boiling water for 20 minutes until tender. Cut and drain.

3 Cook the beef over a high heat then toss with the vegetables, noodles and dressing. Serve in bowls.

dressing

1 Mix together the chilli sauce, ginger, lime or lemon rind and juice and water.

Serves 4

one-pan bolognaise

2 tblsp oil
500–600 grams **Quality Mark Minced Beef**
2 onions, peeled and diced
1–2 tsp minced garlic
¼ cup tomato paste
150–250 grams mushrooms, sliced
400 gram can **Wattie's Chunky Tomatoes with Roasted Garlic**
2½ cups beef stock
1½ cups or 150 grams broken dried spaghetti or fettuccine
2 cups frozen **Wattie's Freshlock™ International Vegetable Mix**
salt and pepper to season

1 Heat the oil in a frying pan and brown the mince over a high heat. Set aside.

2 Cook the onion and garlic for 1 minute then stir in the tomato paste. Cook for 2–3 minutes.

3 Return the mince to the pan with the mushrooms, tomatoes, stock and spaghetti. Stir, cover and simmer for 10 minutes. Stir in the frozen vegetables and cook for a further 5 minutes. Season.

Serves 4

roast beef with mushroom sauce

beef
1 tblsp oil
750 gram piece beef Scotch fillet
2 tsp horseradish cream
2 tsp prepared mustard
2 tsp brown sugar
chopped parsley, or ground black pepper for garnish

mushroom sauce
1 onion, peeled and finely chopped
1 tblsp oil
1 tsp minced fresh garlic
½ cup port or medium-sweet sherry
1 cup beef stock
4 flat (field) mushrooms, chopped
220 gram can **Wattie's Sliced Mushrooms in Butter Sauce**

beef
1. If wished, tie the Scotch fillet with string. This helps keep the fillet in good shape. Heat the oil in a frying pan and when very hot add the beef. Cook quickly over a high heat, browning the fillet evenly on all sides. Transfer to a plate.
2. Mix together the horseradish, mustard and brown sugar. Spread this mixture on the top and down the sides of the meat.
3. Place in a 220°C oven, turn down to 200°C and cook for 40 minutes. Set aside to rest for 10 minutes before carving. Scatter with chopped parsley or grind over plenty of black pepper if wished, before serving with mushroom sauce.

mushroom sauce
1. Cook the onion in the oil in a saucepan over a moderate heat for about 5 minutes until the onion is soft. Add the garlic and cook for a further minute.
2. Add the port or sherry and simmer until reduced by half. Add the beef stock, chopped mushrooms and sliced mushrooms in sauce. Simmer for 10 minutes.

Serves **6**

cheesy-topped steak and kidney pies

750 gram–1 kg chuck steak, well trimmed
250 grams beef kidney
about ¼ cup seasoned flour
4–6 tblsp oil
2 onions, peeled and finely chopped
¼ cup **Wattie's Tomato Paste**
200 grams mushrooms, diced

1 cup red wine
1 cup beef stock
salt and pepper to season
2 x 400 gram blocks savoury short pastry, defrosted but very cold
1 cup grated cheddar cheese

1. Cut the steak into 3 cm pieces. Remove any white core from the kidney and then cut into 2 cm pieces. Toss the beef and kidney in the seasoned flour to coat.
2. Heat half the oil in a flameproof casserole and begin to brown the beef and kidney in batches. Set aside.
3. Add the remaining oil to the casserole, add the onion and cook until just lightly coloured.
4. Add the tomato paste and cook for 2 minutes. Return the meat to the casserole with the mushrooms, red wine and beef stock. Stir well, season with pepper and then cover.
5. Cook at 160°C for 1½–2 hours or until the meat is tender. Season with salt and pepper.
6. Transfer the mixture to 6 x 1-cup-capacity pie dishes.* Grate the pastry and cheese and toss together. Scatter the grated pastry and cheese mix on top of the pies.
7. Bake at 200°C at the top of the oven for 15–20 minutes or just until the pastry is golden and cooked. Serve with your favourite vegetables.

Serves 6

Make one large pie if wished.

cajun lamb steaks with grilled summer salad

steaks

½ tsp each dried oregano, basil and thyme
½ tsp ground black pepper
2 tblsp finely chopped fresh parsley
2 tsp Tabasco sauce
2 tblsp **Wattie's Tomato Sauce**
1 tblsp lemon juice
1 tsp minced fresh garlic
4 small-medium-sized Quality Mark Leg of Lamb Steaks
olive oil spray

salad

2 red peppers, quartered
4 stalks celery, diced
250 grams mushrooms, sliced
400 gram can **Wattie's Cajun-Style Tomatoes**
2 tblsp picked oregano leaves

steaks

1 In a bowl mix together the oregano, basil, thyme, pepper, parsley, Tabasco, tomato sauce, lemon juice and garlic.

2 Flatten the lamb steaks lightly with a mallet and place in a shallow dish. Spread the marinade over the steaks, turning them to coat. Allow to marinate for 30 minutes to 1 hour.

3 Heat a dash of oil in a frying pan and cook the steaks for 2–3 minutes each side until medium. Serve with summer salad.

salad

1 Grill the pepper quarters until blackened. Cool. Peel and cut into 3 cm pieces.

2 In a bowl, toss together the peppers, celery and mushrooms with the tomatoes and oregano.

Serves **4**

lamb kebabs

lamb kebabs

500 grams Quality Mark Diced Lamb
¼ cup oil (olive is nice here)
1 tblsp chopped fresh rosemary
1 tsp minced fresh garlic
black pepper to season
2 courgettes, thickly sliced
1 large red pepper, diced
about 16 button mushrooms

couscous

3 cups boiling water
1½ cups couscous
½ cup chopped black olives
¼–½ cup **Eta Italian Vinaigrette**
¼ cup chopped basil (optional)

1. Toss the lamb with the oil, rosemary, garlic and a good seasoning of pepper. Marinate for 10–15 minutes.
2. Thread courgette onto skewers alternately with the lamb, red pepper and mushrooms.
3. Fan grill at 180°C for 8–10 minutes, turning occasionally to ensure even browning.
4. Pour the boiling water over the couscous and stand for 5 minutes. Fluff the couscous with a fork and add the olives, dressing and basil if using and season. Serve the lamb kebabs on the couscous.

Serves 4–5

shepherd's pie

500 grams Quality Mark Minced Lean Lamb
2 onions, peeled and finely chopped
1 tblsp oil
¼ cup tomato paste
2 tsp minced garlic
420 gram can **Wattie's Baked Beans**
1 cup beef or vegetable stock
2–3 cups frozen **Wattie's Freshlock™ International Vegetables**
750 grams (about 6) potatoes, mashed and slightly warm
½ cup grated cheddar cheese

1. Brown the mince and onion in the hot oil. Stir in the tomato paste and cook for 5–6 minutes.
2. Stir in the garlic, beans and beef or vegetable stock. Cover and simmer for 10 minutes. Add the frozen vegetables and stir to mix.
3. Transfer the mixture to a dish and top with the mashed potato and grated cheese.
4. Bake at 180°C for 30–35 minutes.

Serves 4–6

lamb provençale

4–6 Quality Mark Lamb Shoulder Steaks or Chops
1 tblsp oil
1 onion, peeled and finely diced
2 stalks celery, trimmed and finely diced
400 gram pouch **Wattie's Simply Cuisine Tuscan Pasta Sauce**

1 cup red wine or beef stock
300 gram can **Craig's Four Bean Mix in Brine**, well drained
12 olives, black or stuffed
¼ cup chopped celery leaves to garnish (optional)

1 Trim any excess fat from the lamb steaks or chops.

2 Heat the oil in a lidded frying pan and brown the chops evenly on both sides. Add the onion, celery, pasta sauce, wine or beef stock and beans. Cover and simmer gently for 40 minutes.

3 Add the olives and celery, if using, 5 minutes before the end of cooking time.

4 Serve garnished with chopped fresh herbs, mashed potatoes and your favourite greens.

Serves 4

rogan josh

1 kg **Quality Mark Boneless Lean Shoulder Lamb**
dash oil
2 onions, peeled and finely sliced
2 tomatoes, chopped
415 gram can **Wattie's Rogan Josh Curry Sauce**
yoghurt and chopped fresh coriander to accompany

1. Trim any excess fat from the lamb. Cut the meat into large, 3 cm pieces.
2. Heat the oil in a large, lidded frying pan until hot. Add the lamb and brown quickly.
3. Add the sliced onion, tomatoes and curry sauce. Bring to the boil, cover and simmer for 15 minutes, then remove the lid and simmer for a further 15 minutes.
4. Allow to stand for 5 minutes before garnishing with yoghurt and chopped coriander and serve with your favourite Indian-style vegetables.

Serves 4–5

curried lamb
with ginger mash

500 grams **Quality Mark Lean Leg Lamb Steaks**
dash oil
¼ cup **Wattie's Tomato Paste**
1 leek, trimmed, rinsed and finely chopped
1 carrot, peeled and finely chopped
415 gram can **Wattie's Rogan Josh** or **Madras Curry Sauce**
750 grams kumara, peeled and chopped
butter and milk for mashing
1 tsp ground ginger
salt and pepper to season

1. Cut the lamb steaks into 1 cm dice. Heat the oil in a frying pan and brown the meat over a high heat. Add the tomato paste and cook for 2–3 minutes, stirring until the paste becomes much darker in colour but not burnt.
2. Stir in the leek, carrot and curry sauce. Lower the heat, cover and simmer for 10 minutes.
3. Cook the kumara in boiling, salted water until tender. Drain and mash with a knob of butter and a good pour of milk. Add the ground ginger, season with salt and pepper and beat until smooth.
4. Divide the curry among 4 individual serving dishes and pile the ginger and kumara mash on top.
5. Bake at 200°C for 10 minutes until piping hot.

Serves 4

lamb korma curry

750 grams Quality Mark Boneless Lean
 Shoulder Lamb, diced
2–3 tblsp oil
1 large onion, peeled and chopped
1 each red and green pepper, cored and roughly chopped
415 gram can **Wattie's Korma Curry Sauce**

$1/2$ cup cream or coconut cream

to accompany
4–6 poppadums
2 bananas, sliced
a little desiccated coconut

1. Brown the lamb in the oil in a lidded frying-pan for 10 minutes. Set aside.
2. Add the onion to the pan and cook over a moderate heat for 5 minutes. Return the lamb to the pan with the peppers and curry sauce and stir well. Cover and simmer for 20–30 minutes or until tender.
3. Add the cream or coconut cream and warm through.
4. Cook 2–3 poppadums in the microwave at one time for 1 minute until crisp. Repeat with the remaining poppadums. Toss the banana slices with the desiccated coconut.
5. Serve the curry over steamed rice garnished with toasted, shredded coconut if desired. Have the poppadums and the banana slices on the side.

Serves 4

satay lamb with crispy noodles

500 grams Quality Mark Lamb Steaks (2 large or 4 small steaks)
1 tblsp oil
1 onion, peeled and finely sliced
3 cups sliced green summer vegetables (asparagus, beans, courgettes or peppers)
425 gram can **Wattie's Satay Stir Fry Sauce**
3–4 cups crispy fried noodles
handful of roasted peanuts to garnish (optional)

1. Trim any fat from the lamb steaks and then cut the meat into very small, 1 cm pieces
2. Heat the oil in a frying pan until very hot and add the meat. Toss quickly over the hot heat to brown and seal the lamb. Do this in two batches to ensure that the lamb does not stew.
3. Add the onion and cook for 1 minute. Add all the summer vegetables and toss for 1–2 minutes.
4. Stir in the satay sauce and cover. Simmer for 4–5 minutes.
5. Toss the crispy fried noodles through the sauce before serving. Serve on a large platter garnished with peanuts if wished.

Serves 4

lamb noodle stir-fry

peanut sauce
½ onion, peeled and finely chopped
¼ cup oil
1 tblsp minced fresh garlic
1 tsp minced chilli
2 tblsp soy sauce
juice 1 lemon or lime
¼ cup brown sugar
375 gram jar **Eta Crunchy Peanut Butter**

stir-fry
200–300 grams egg noodles or thin spaghetti
300 grams Quality Mark Boneless Leg Lamb Steaks, well trimmed
1 tblsp soy sauce
1 tsp minced fresh garlic
good pinch nutmeg (optional)
2 tblsp oil
2 cups shredded cabbage or 2–3 bok choy, washed and sliced
½ cup chicken stock

peanut sauce
1. Cook the onion, garlic and chilli in the hot oil in a frying pan until softened.
2. Stir in the soy sauce, lemon or lime juice, brown sugar and peanut butter. Once mixed, remove from the heat.

stir-fry
1. Cook the egg noodles or spaghetti in boiling, salted water. Drain and keep warm.
2. Toss the lamb with the soy sauce, garlic and nutmeg and stand for 10 minutes. Heat the oil in a non-stick frying pan and quickly cook the lamb over a high heat. Set aside. Add the vegetables to the hot pan and toss to cook. Add the lamb, noodles, ¼ cup of the peanut sauce and the chicken stock and toss to mix. Serve immediately.

Serves 4

Note: This peanut sauce makes a great dip. Keep refrigerated.

turkish lamb casserole

750 grams Quality Mark Leg of Lamb
5–6 tblsp oil (olive is nice here)
2 onions, peeled and diced
1 yellow pepper, cored and diced
1–1½ tblsp minced fresh garlic
¼ cup **Wattie's Tomato Paste**
2 tblsp flour
1 tblsp ground cumin
400 gram can **Wattie's Italian Seasoned Tomatoes**
310 gram can chickpeas, well drained

1½ cups beef stock
3–4 sprigs thyme
1 small to medium-sized aubergine
2 courgettes, sliced

to accompany
non-fat yoghurt
chopped fresh coriander
couscous

1 Cut the lamb into large, 3–4 cm dice. Heat 1 tablespoon of the oil in an ovenproof casserole and when hot, brown the lamb in batches.

2 Heat a second tablespoon of oil in the casserole and add the onion and pepper. Cook for 5 minutes before adding the garlic and tomato paste. Cook the tomato paste, stirring regularly until it becomes a deep brown-red colour.

3 Add the flour and ground cumin and cook for 1 minute. Return the lamb to the pan with the tomatoes, chickpeas, beef stock and thyme. Bring to the boil, cover and transfer to the oven.

4 Cook at 160°C for 1½ hours.

5 Cut the aubergine into thick, finger-sized pieces. Heat the remaining oil and quickly brown the aubergine on all sides. Add to the casserole with the courgettes and cook for a further 30 minutes.

6 Serve on couscous, garnished with yoghurt and chopped coriander if wished.

Serves **6**

braised lamb shanks in merlot with figs

6 lamb shanks
2 large onions, peeled and finely chopped
2 stalks celery, trimmed and finely chopped
12–20 black olives
2–4 tblsp capers
2 cups dried figs, halved
2 tblsp fresh rosemary
1 tsp ground black pepper
6 cloves garlic, crushed but not peeled
750 ml bottle Merlot
about 2 tblsp oil
¼ cup **Wattie's Tomato Paste**
1 cup stock (beef or chicken)
salt and pepper to season

1 In a deep dish, put the lamb shanks, onions, celery, olives, capers, dried figs, rosemary, black pepper and garlic and pour over the wine. Cover and marinate in the refrigerator overnight or for at least 4 hours. **(a)**

2 Remove the shanks from the marinade and set aside. Heat the oil in a frying pan and brown the shanks on all sides. **(b)** Transfer the shanks to a casserole.

3 Add the tomato paste to the pan and stir over a moderate heat until it becomes a deep reddish-brown colour. Add the stock and bring to the boil. **(c)**

4 Pour over the lamb shanks and add the reserved marinade ingredients. **(d)**

5 Cover the casserole and cook at 160°C for 2–2½ hours until the meat is almost falling off the bone. Season with salt and pepper if wished. Serve with roughly mashed potatoes and fresh greens.

Serves 4-6

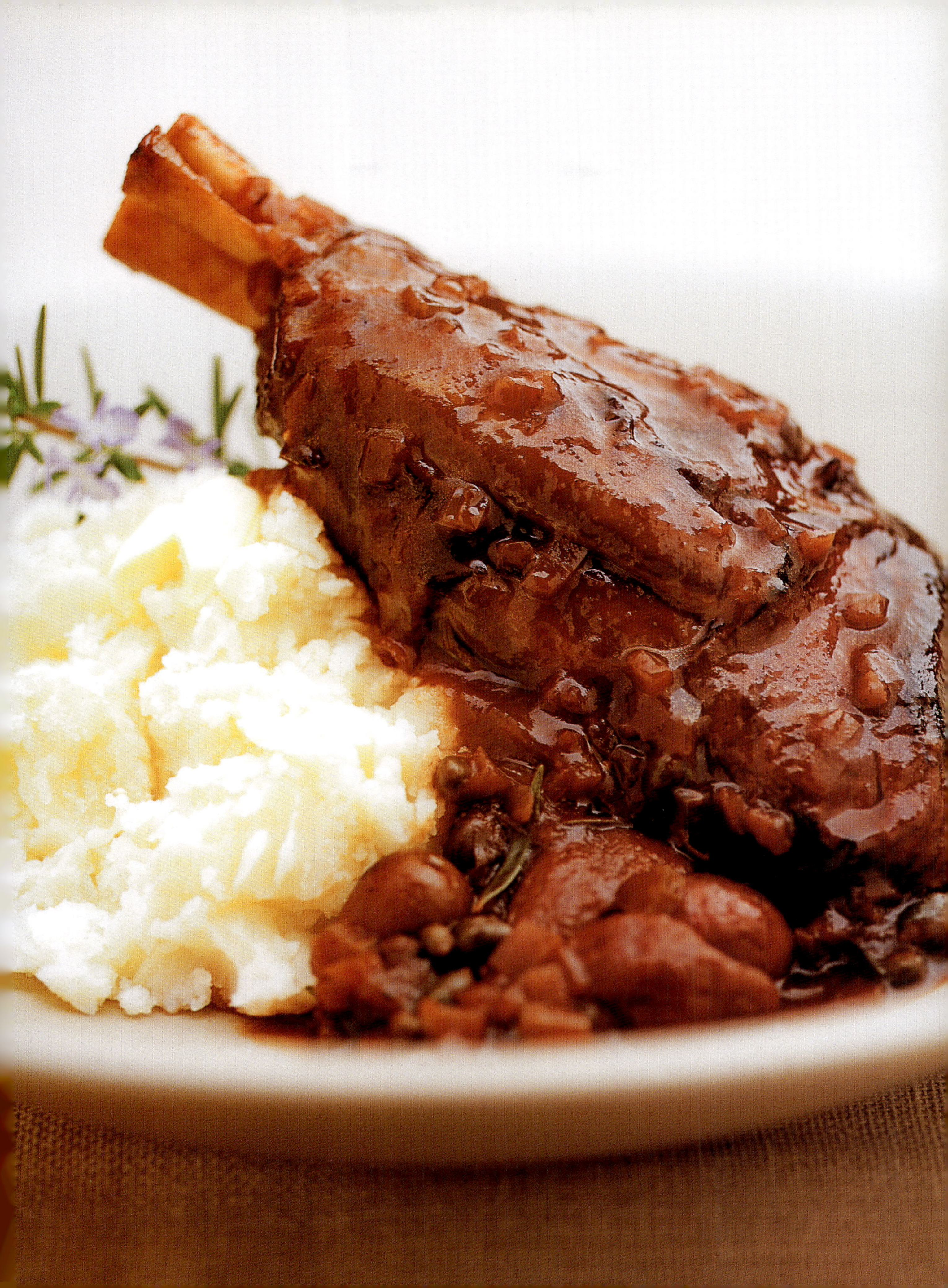

bacon-wrapped lamb chops

1 cup fresh white or wholemeal breadcrumbs
2 tblsp chopped fresh parsley or coriander
300 gram jar **Wattie's Bit on the Side Corn Canyon Salsa**

8 loin lamb chops
8 **Kiwi Bacon Strips**
Wattie's Potato Croquettes (optional)

1. Mix the breadcrumbs and parsley or coriander with 6 tablespoons of the salsa.
2. Using a sharp knife (a paring knife is fine), cut down either side of each chop bone to remove the bone. You will be left with a small nut of lamb fillet and the larger, boneless loin.
3. Place 1 tablespoon of the salsa stuffing in the centre. Place the small nut of lamb beside it and roll up to enclose and make a neat round.
4. Wrap a bacon strip around the outside of the lamb and secure with a toothpick. Repeat with the remaining chops and stuffing.
5. Place the lamb on a foil-lined baking tray with the potato croquettes if using.
6. Fan grill towards the top of a 200°C oven for 12–15 minutes, turning once.
7. Serve with the remaining salsa and your favourite vegetables or salad.

Serves 4

minted kofta kebabs

1 onion, peeled and finely diced
2 tsp minced garlic
500 grams Quality Mark Lean Minced Lamb
¼–½ cup finely chopped mint
¼ cup chopped fresh coriander
1 tsp each ground cumin, pepper, coriander and salt
1 egg
2–3 tomatoes, sliced

1. In a bowl mix together the onion, garlic, minced lamb, mint, fresh coriander, cumin, pepper, ground coriander, salt and egg.
2. Mould the mixture onto 6 bamboo skewers or chopsticks, squeezing them tightly so that the mixture will not fall off during cooking. Refrigerate for at least 1 hour before cooking.
3. Barbecue or grill for 15–20 minutes, turning to ensure even cooking.
4. Serve with Barley Tabouleh, on sliced tomatoes and accompanied with the Yoghurt Mint Sauce. If wished, add a few black olives, mint leaves and a drizzle of olive oil when serving.

barley tabouleh

1 cup uncooked barley
1 cup Eta Italian Vinaigrette
½ cup chopped fresh mint
1 cup chopped parsley
1 tsp salt
freshly ground black pepper (lots of it)

1. Cook the barley in plenty of boiling, salted water for about 35 minutes until tender. Set aside to cool.
2. In a large bowl, combine the barley, vinaigrette, mint, parsley, salt, and plenty of pepper to season. Allow to stand for 1 hour before serving. Serve cool but not chilled.

yoghurt mint sauce

1 cup non-fat, plain yoghurt
1 tblsp lemon juice
¼ cup minced mint
salt and pepper to taste
¼ cup grated cucumber (optional)

1. Blend together all the ingredients except cucumber. Add cucumber if wished.

Serves 4–6

spicy lamb and potato pasties

1 tblsp oil
1 onion, diced
500 grams Quality Mark Lean Minced Lamb
1 tsp each ground coriander and cumin
½ tsp cinnamon, salt and pepper
½ cup **Wattie's Tomato Paste**
500 grams cooked potatoes, finely diced
1 cup beef stock or water
5 sheets pre-rolled savoury pastry
milk or beaten egg to glaze

1. Heat the oil in a frying pan and pan-fry the onion and lamb over a moderately high heat until well browned.

2. Add the spices and tomato paste and cook for a further 2 minutes. Stir in the potato, stock or water and simmer for 10 minutes or until the potato is cooked.

3. Use a bread and butter plate to cut 5 circles from the pastry sheets. Re-roll off cuts and cut a further circle.

4. Divide the lamb mixture among the circles of pastry. Brush the pastry edges with milk and bring together, pressing firmly to seal. Brush pasties with milk to glaze.

5. Place on a greased tray and bake at 200°C at the top of the oven for 20–25 minutes until golden.

Makes 6 pasties

savoury mince roll-ups

1 tblsp oil
1 onion, peeled and diced
500 grams minced Lamb or Beef
¼ cup rice
½ cup water
545 gram can **Wattie's Just Add Country French Mince**
2–3 cups chopped vegetables (use broccoli, carrot, etc)
6 tortilla burritos
1½ cups grated edam cheese

1. Heat the oil in a lidded frying pan and cook the onion and minced beef or lamb until browned.

2. Add the rice, water, sauce and vegetables. Cover and simmer for 10 minutes until vegetables are tender. Remove from the heat.

3. Divide the mixture evenly between the tortillas and roll up. Place in a well-greased, lasagne-style baking dish and sprinkle over the cheese.

4. Bake at 200°C for 15 minutes until the cheese has melted and browned. Serve hot with a salad.

Serves 4

variation
- *Substitute the rice with ½ cup crushed pasta.*

lamb pitas with tomato yoghurt chilli sauce

lamb pitas

500 grams Quality Mark Lean Lamb Leg Steaks
salt and pepper
2 tblsp oil
4 rounds of Lebanese breads
1 cup hummus
2–3 handfuls salad greens or herb leaves
2 cups of your favourite prepared coleslaw
¼ cup chopped mint

tomato yoghurt chilli sauce

½ cup **Wattie's Tomato Purée**
½ cup plain, unsweetened yoghurt
1 tsp minced chilli (optional)

lamb pitas

1 Slice the lamb thinly. Season well with salt and pepper.

2 Heat the oil in a frying pan and sear the lamb over a high heat, stirring until it is cooked through. Put aside.

3 In a clean pan heat the Lebanese breads one at a time until warm.

4 To assemble, spread each Lebanese bread with hummus, top with salad greens or herb leaves, coleslaw, cooked lamb, mint and a spoonful of Tomato Yoghurt Chilli Sauce. Roll up lightly to secure the filling. Serve warm.

tomato yoghurt chilli sauce

1 Combine all the ingredients in a bowl.

Serves **4**

quick winter roast lamb

2 Quality Mark Loins of Lamb (each with 6–7 chops)
Lea & Perrins Worcestershire Sauce
1 tsp minced garlic
pepper for seasoning
2 onions, peeled and sliced
2 parsnips, peeled and thickly sliced
250 grams pumpkin, sliced
dash oil
½ 750 gram packet frozen **Wattie's Freshlock™ Whole Baby Green Beans**

1. Score the lamb loins on the skin side and season well with Worcestershire sauce. Turn over and season the meat well with Worcestershire sauce, garlic and pepper. Tie the flap securely with string.
2. Toss the onion, parsnip and pumpkin in the dash of oil and place in a shallow roasting dish. Sit the lamb loins on top.
3. Bake at 220°C (fan-bake 200°C) for 35 minutes.
4. Transfer the lamb to a plate and sprinkle the baby beans into the baking dish, toss and return to the oven for 5 minutes. Remove from the oven and toss the vegetables with a knob of butter. Season with salt and pepper.
5. Carve the lamb into chops and serve over the hot vegetables, accompanied by your favourite sauce or gravy.

Serves 4–6

pork and ham

{pork and ham} tips and hints

1 Pork (uncooked) should be stored in the coolest part of the refrigerator. If you plan to keep pork for more than 2–3 days before cooking, store it in the freezer. Defrost in the refrigerator always.

2 Pork cuts best for casseroles include leg or shoulder steak **(a)**, rump **(b)**, diced steak **(c)**, pieces, chops **(d)** and slices **(e)**.

3 Pork cuts best for grilling, pan-frying or barbecuing include butterfly steaks **(f)**, Scotch fillet steaks **(g)**, medallions **(h)**, schnitzel **(i)**, and mince patties **(j)**.

4 Trim Pork is a registered trademark of New Zealand Pork and can only be applied to specific pork cuts that are 100 percent New Zealand grown pork, boneless, skinless and trimmed to less than 5 mm of fat. New Zealand Pork is not genetically modified.

5 Pork mince made into meatballs or hamburgers does not need an egg to bind the meat together.

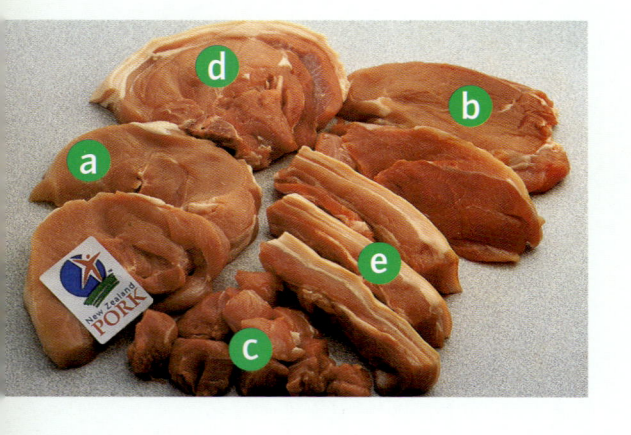

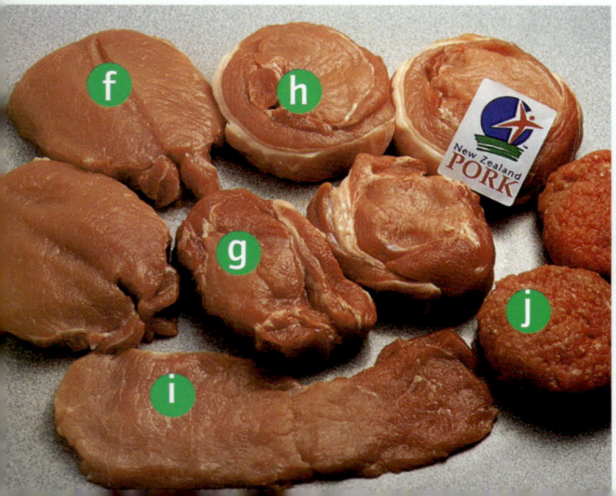

6 As a general guide allow 125 grams uncooked, boneless pork per person. When buying a roast with a bone in the cut, allow 150–175 grams of uncooked weight.

7 If you are marinating meat before stir-frying, be sure to drain the meat well before stir-frying. If the marinade has a high sugar content level, do not cook over too high a heat as the meat will burn before it cooks. For even cooking, cut the meat into the same size pieces.

8 Pork marries very well with fruit flavours. Fry peaches, apricots, pears, boysenberries, cranberries, blackcurrants, apples and oranges for great variation.

9 Pork is cooked when it reaches an internal temperature of 71°C. For well done pork this is 76°C. If you do not have a thermometer, pierce the pork with a skewer at the thickest part; if the juices run clear the pork is cooked. If they are still bloody, continue cooking.

10 To achieve fantastic crackling, follow these simple steps:

1 Make sure the rind is well scored.
2 Rub the rind liberally with oil and salt.
3 Place the roast of pork initially into a hot oven (220°C) for 15–20 minutes, then lower the temperature until the meat is cooked.
4 Rest before carving.

mexican marinated pork loin chops

2 tblsp oil
2 tblsp lemon juice
2 tsp minced fresh garlic
2 tblsp chopped fresh oregano or 2 tsp dried
2 tblsp chopped fresh coriander or parsley
1/2 tsp ground allspice
1/2 tsp ground or minced chilli
salt and pepper to season
4–6 New Zealand Pork Chops

1. In a bowl mix together the oil, lemon juice, garlic, oregano, coriander or parsley, allspice and chilli with a good seasoning of salt and pepper.

2. Place 4–6 pork chops in a dish and pour over the marinade. Turn to coat. Cover and refrigerate for at least 1 hour or up to overnight.

3. Cook the pork chops over a moderately hot barbecue, turning occasionally, for 7–8 minutes until the pork is well browned and just cooked. To test if the pork chops are cooked, pierce the meat near the bone and if the juices run clear, the chops are cooked.

4. Serve the pork with barbecued Wattie's Freshlock Corn Cobs, a little butter and plenty of summer salads.

Serves 4–6

mediterranean meatballs on pasta

500 grams minced pork
1/2 cup chopped fresh herbs or 2 tblsp dried
1 onion, peeled and finely chopped
1 slice white bread, crumbed
salt and pepper to season
2 tblsp oil or clarified butter
1/2 cup red wine or chicken stock or water
400 gram can **Wattie's Mediterranean Tomatoes**

garnish
grated parmesan cheese
olives
fresh herbs (optional)

1. In a bowl mix together the pork, herbs, onion and bread. Season. Roll the mixture into 24 balls.

2. Heat the oil in a frying pan and cook the meatballs until they are evenly browned all over. Add the red wine and simmer for 5 minutes. Stir in the tomatoes. Cover and simmer for 20 minutes.

3. Serve meatballs on pasta, garnished with cheese, olives and herbs if wished.

Serves 4

pork with courgettes

grated rind and juice 1 orange
¼ cup honey
2 tsp Chinese five spice powder
1 kg thick, sliced pork slices
dash oil
4 courgettes, trimmed and sliced
425 gram can **Wattie's Sweet Chilli Stir Fry Sauce**

garnish (optional)
150 grams cooked prawns
few toasted cashew nuts

1. Mix the orange rind and juice with the honey and five spice powder. Toss the pork in this mixture and leave to marinate for up to 8 hours — the longer the better. (I use a Snaplock bag to marinate the ingredients.)

2. Grill the pork slices under a high heat for 10 minutes each side or until well cooked and crispy. Cut into 1 cm-wide slices.

3. Heat the oil in a frying pan and quickly cook the courgettes over a moderately high heat until browned, but do not overcook. Add the stir-fry sauce to the pork and toss to heat all ingredients through.

4. Serve garnished with the prawns and cashew nuts if wished.

Serves 4

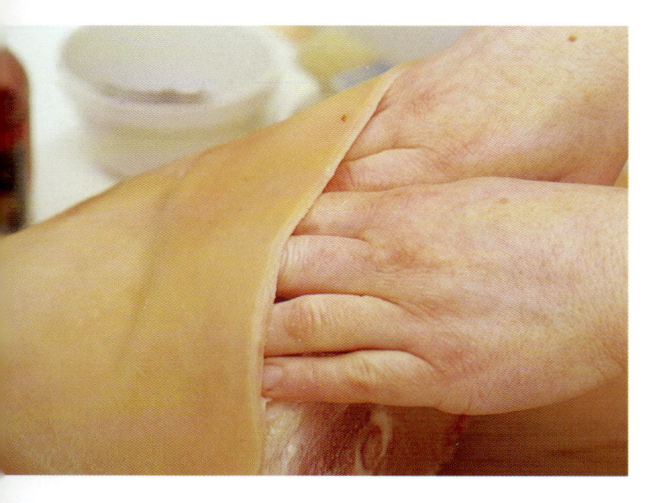

oriental christmas ham with plum salsa

ham
½ cooked New Zealand Ham on the Bone
½ cup **Wattie's Bit on the Side Oriental Plum Sauce**
about ¼ cup whole cloves

plum salsa
4 ripe plums, halved and stoned
2 spring onions, trimmed and finely chopped
¼ cup **Wattie's Bit on the Side Oriental Plum Sauce**
1 tsp minced fresh ginger
2 tblsp chopped fresh mint
pinch salt

ham

1 Carefully lift the skin from the cooked ham. To do this, run your clean fingers between the skin and the ham and it will come away easily. **(a)**

2 Using a sharp knife, score the fat in a criss-cross diamond pattern, but only as deep as the fat level. **(b)**

3 If wished, place a whole clove at the corners of each diamond. **(c)**

4 Spread the ham with the ½ cup plum sauce. **(d)**

5 To have the ham hot, cook at 160°C for 10 minutes per 500 grams. To glaze the ham only, bake at 180°C for 35–40 minutes.

plum salsa

1 Dice the plums finely.

2 In a bowl mix together the plums, spring onion, plum sauce, ginger and mint. Season with a pinch of salt.

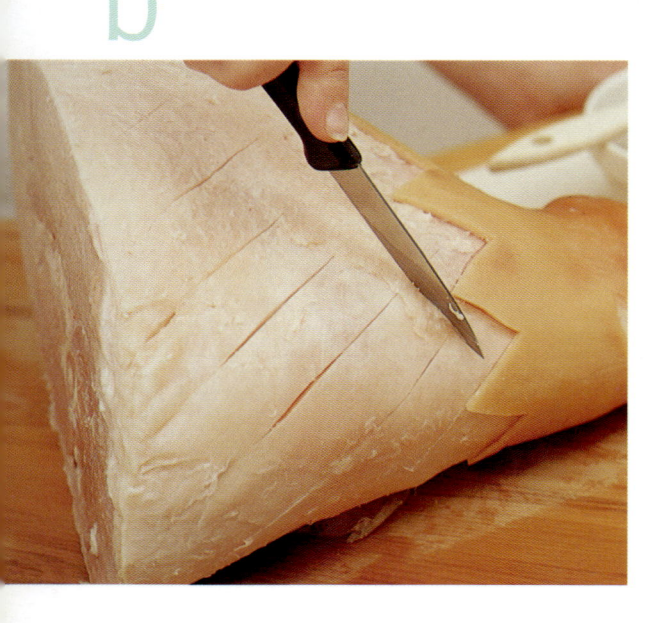

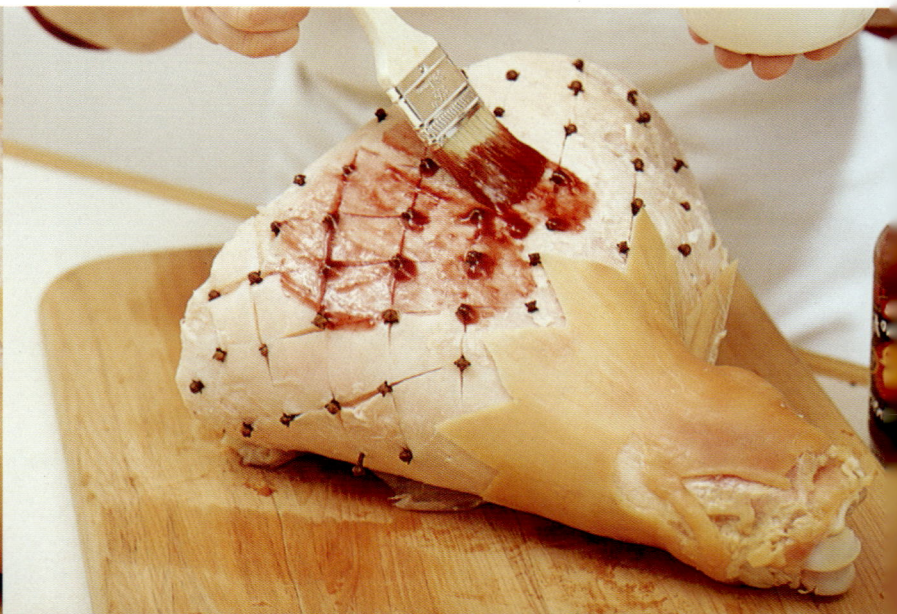

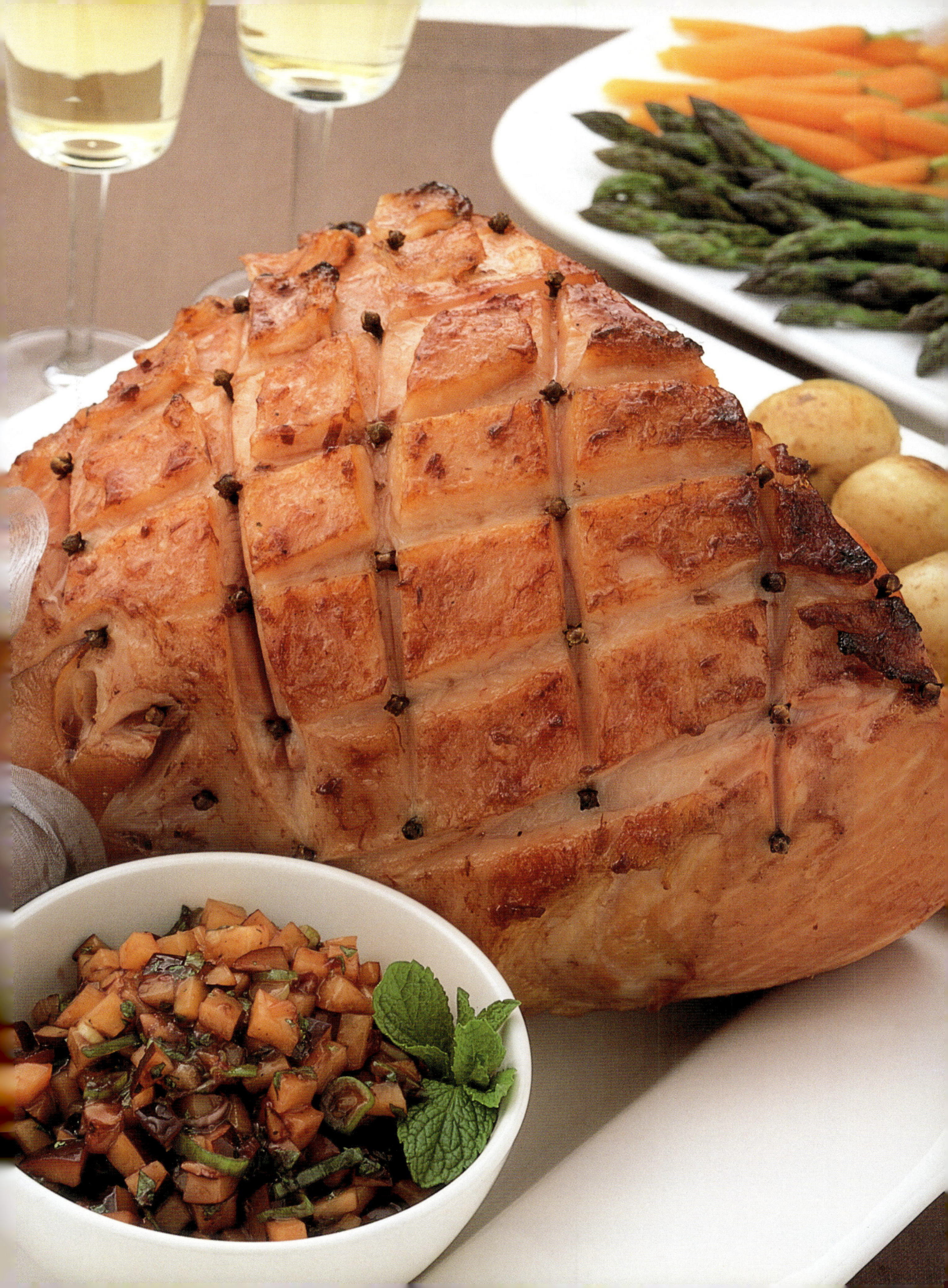

sausage hot pot

500 grams sausage meat
¼ cup chopped parsley
¼ cup **Wattie's Tomato Sauce**
pepper to season
1 apple, peeled and grated
1 egg
oil
545 gram can **Wattie's Just Add Brown Onion Sausages Simmer Sauce**

1. In a bowl mix together the sausage meat, parsley, tomato sauce, pepper, apple and egg.
2. Using wet hands roll into 20 even-shaped balls.
3. Heat a dash of oil in a lidded frying pan and brown the sausage balls evenly on all sides.
4. Add the brown onion sauce, stir, cover and simmer for 30 minutes over a low heat.
5. Serve with your favourite winter vegetables.

Serves 4

ham and courgette pasta

4 cups shell pasta (large or small)
dash oil to pan-fry
4 large courgettes, trimmed and grated
5–6 spring onions, trimmed and finely chopped
2–3 ham steaks, diced
420 gram can **Wattie's Creamy Condensed Chicken Soup**
½ cup milk or chicken stock

1. Cook the pasta in boiling, salted water for 12–15 minutes until 'al dente' or almost cooked. Drain well and keep warm.
2. Heat the oil in a frying pan, add the courgettes and spring onion and cook over a moderately high heat for about 5 minutes, stirring regularly.
3. Add the ham, chicken soup and milk or stock. Simmer for 3–4 minutes until hot.
4. Toss the well-drained pasta through the sauce and serve with garlic bread to the side.

Serves 4

golden plum pork loin chops

chops
12–16 prunes
2 tblsp port or red wine
6–8 lean, boneless loin pork chops
½ cup **Wattie's Bit on the Side Oriental Plum Sauce**

topping
2 spring onions
½ cup toasted cashew nuts (preferably unsalted)

1. Soak the prunes in the port or red wine for about 30 minutes.
2. Arrange the pork chops and prunes in a 6-cup-capacity, lasagne-style baking dish. Spread over the plum sauce. Bake at 200°C for 25 minutes. Chop the spring onions and cashews and sprinkle over the pork just before serving with your favourite vegetables.

Serves **4–6**

spicy pork and bean tagine

1 kg lean pork
2 onions, peeled and chopped
2 tsp minced fresh garlic
½ cup parsley sprigs
about 2 tblsp chopped fresh coriander
1 tsp ground turmeric
1 tsp ground cumin
½ tsp each salt and white pepper
50 grams butter
1½ cups chicken stock
500 gram bag frozen **Wattie's Freshlock™ Broad Beans**
20 stuffed green olives
1 red pepper, deseeded and finely sliced (optional)

1. Cut the pork into 3 cm pieces and place in a large bowl.
2. In a food processor put the onion, garlic, parsley, coriander, turmeric, cumin, salt and white pepper. Process until smooth and then pour over the pork. Toss to coat, cover and refrigerate for 4 hours.
3. Heat the butter in a frying pan and brown the pork on all sides. Transfer to a casserole.
4. Add any remaining marinade liquid to the pan with the chicken stock and bring to the boil. Pour over the pork and cover.
5. Cook at 160°C for 1 hour.
6. If wished, blanch and peel the broad beans. Add to the tagine with the olives and pepper if using. Cook for a further 10 minutes until the beans are hot and tender.
7. Serve over couscous, garnished with pinenuts and sprigs of fresh parsley or coriander if wished.

Serves **6–8**

sweet apple and pork braise

500 grams New Zealand Trim Pork Leg Steaks
1 tblsp oil
2 small onions, peeled and diced
2–3 stalks celery, trimmed and finely chopped
1 tsp minced fresh garlic
½ cup raisins or sultanas
1 tblsp chopped fresh sage or 1 tsp dried
½–1 300 gram bottle **Wattie's Bit on the Side Absolutely Apple Sauce**
½ cup chicken stock or water
pepper to season
sage leaves to garnish

1. Cut the pork into 3 cm pieces. Heat the oil in a lidded frying pan and when very hot quickly brown the pork pieces on all sides.
2. Add the onion, celery, garlic, raisins or sultanas, sage, apple sauce and stock or water. Season with pepper and stir. (If only using ½ a bottle of Apple Sauce, add an extra ½ cup of stock or water.)
3. Cover and simmer on top of the stove over a low heat for 30 minutes or until the pork is tender.
4. Serve over mashed kumara or potato garnished with extra sage leaves.

Serves **4**

spicy plum pork spareribs

2 kg pork spareribs
425 gram can **Wattie's Spicy Plum Stir Fry Sauce**
¼ cup sweet sherry

1. Cut down between the bones of the spareribs and place the spareribs in a large shallow dish.
2. Purée the contents of the spicy plum sauce in a blender or processor with the sherry.
3. Pour over the spareribs and toss well to coat evenly. Cover, refrigerate and leave overnight or for at least 4 hours to marinate.
4. Place on a rack above a foil-lined tray. Bake at 190°C for 1–1¼ hours or until the spareribs are well cooked and crispy.

Serves **6**

spicy pork and bean tagine

rolled roast belly pork with peach stuffing

pork

410 gram can **Wattie's Peach Slices in Syrup**, well drained
1 cup fresh white breadcrumbs
½ cup finely chopped or ground pecans
2–3 pieces crystallised ginger or papaya, diced (optional)
75 grams butter, softened
grated rind 1 orange
1 tsp ground allspice or mixed spice

1.5 kg piece belly of pork, scored
2 tblsp oil or lemon juice
1 tblsp salt

peach salsa

½ red onion, peeled and diced
2 tblsp honey
2 tblsp chopped fresh mint
1 tblsp lemon juice
2 tblsp oil

pork

1. Dice the peaches and mix ½ cup together with the breadcrumbs, pecans, ginger or papaya, butter, orange rind and allspice or mixed spice. Place the pork skin side down and spread the filling down the centre lengthwise.

2. Bring the pork together to enclose the stuffing and secure with string or skewers. Rub the oil or lemon juice and salt into the pork skin.

3. Place in a hot, 220°C oven for 15 minutes and then lower the temperature to 170°C and cook for a further 1–1¼ hours. The crackling should be crisp and the meat cooked. When pierced with a meat fork the juice should run clear; if pink continue cooking.

4. Once the meat has rested for 10–15 minutes, carve and serve with a salad and peach salsa.

peach salsa

1. Mix the remaining diced peaches with the red onion, honey, mint, lemon juice and oil.

Serves **6–8**

tuna
and other fish

{tuna and other fish}
tips and hints

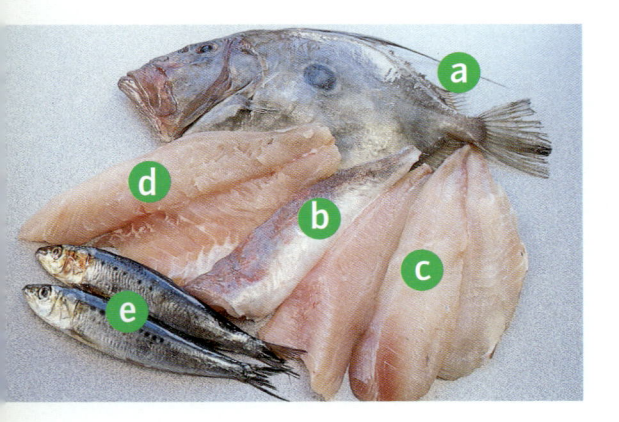

1 Canned tuna is low in fat, unless it has been canned in oil. An excellent source of protein, it can be easily flaked and added to risottos, other rice and pasta dishes, salads, omelettes, etc. Keep a can on hand at all times.

2 Recipes often call for medium- or firm-textured fish. These species have the ability to either hold their shape or flake in thick pieces. They are:

i **Medium-textured fish** — blue cod, John dory (a), lookdown dory, barracuda, garfish, red gurnard (b), deep-sea cod, snapper (c), tarakihi (d), trevally, tuna, warehou, blue and Jack mackerel, skipjack tuna, pilchards and sardines (e).

ii **Firm-textured fish** — ling (f), smooth oreo dory, monkfish, bluenose, alfonsino, groper, black oreo dory, northern kingfish (g), hapuka (h), quinnat salmon, southern bluefin tuna.

3 Some tips to remember when buying fish:
- It's best to buy fish the day you intend to cook it.
- Fish should smell clean and fresh. If it is strong in odour, leave it.
- For whole fish the eyes should be bright, the skin should be bright and have a sheen and the gills bright red.
- Fish bought the day before and kept refrigerated can be refreshed in ice-cold water to which a handful of salt has been added.
- Fish cooking time is determined by the thickness of the fillet. To pan-fry a 2 cm-thick fillet will take 6–7 minutes, while a 3 cm-thick fillet such as salmon will take 10 minutes.
- Cold, leftover fish can be turned into fish cakes.

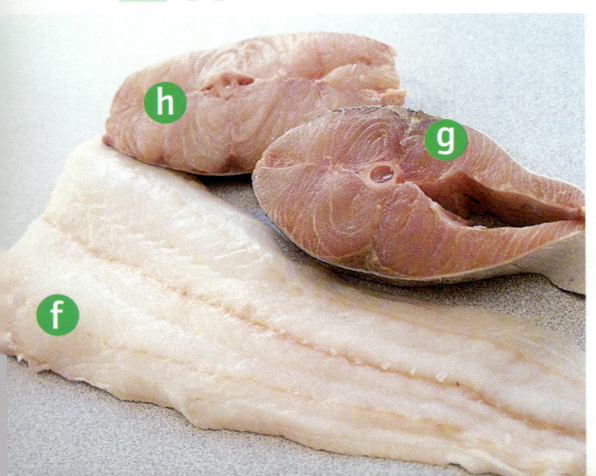

4 Fish is cooked when it is moist and flakes easily. Overcooking causes fish to become dry and unpleasant.

5 When preparing smoked fish to add to a pie or casserole, pull the fish into bite-sized pieces, discarding the bones and skin.

6 Pan-frying foods like fish cakes is best done in a very small amount of clarified butter or oil, in a non-stick pan. Cook over a moderate heat so food can heat through and cook without burning on the outside.

7 Soy sauces are prepared from soy beans, wheat, salt and water. Dark soy sometimes called 'soy superior sauce' is thicker, more richly coloured and sweeter because of the addition of molasses or sugar. Use dark soy in marinades. Light soy sauce is thinner and slightly saltier than dark soy and is best used for dipping. To tell the difference between the soy sauce, turn the bottles upside down and if it is dark soy, it will coat the bottle neck and run down slowly unlike light soy which will run back into the bottle quickly. (See tuna recipes page 142.)

8 Sesame oil is an intense-flavoured oil which should be used with a light hand. Too much is over-powering. Drizzle it over fish before serving. Keep it away from light and heat so it does not go rancid before the contents are used. (See tuna recipes page 142.)

9 Nuts and seeds (including desiccated coconut) should be kept in the freezer. They have a high oil content and can go rancid if left in a warm place. As nuts are low in moisture content, you can re-freeze them. (See tuna recipes page 142.)

coconut fish curry

600 grams thick, firm-textured fish fillets
juice ½ lemon
½ tsp salt
1 tsp minced fresh ginger
1–2 tblsp oil
415 gram can **Wattie's Butter Chicken Curry Sauce**
¼ cup cream or coconut cream
2 tblsp chopped fresh coriander or parsley

1. Cut the fish into 3–4 cm pieces and toss with the lemon juice, salt and ginger. Cover and set aside for 15 minutes.
2. Heat the oil in a lidded frying pan and when hot quickly seal the fish pieces on all sides.
3. Add the curry sauce, cream or coconut cream and coriander or parsley. Cover and simmer for 7–10 minutes until the fish flakes easily and is cooked.
4. Serve the fish over steaming hot rice with your favourite vegetable or salad.

Serves 4

fish provençale

1 tsp garlic
3 tblsp lemon juice
4 tblsp olive oil
750 grams thick, white, medium- or firm-textured fish fillets, diced into 2 cm pieces
1 green and 1 red pepper, grilled, peeled and diced
1 onion, peeled and diced
2 tblsp tomato paste
400 gram can **Wattie's Italian Seasoned Tomatoes**
1 tblsp chopped fresh oregano
½ cup green olives
freshly ground black pepper

1. Combine the garlic, lemon juice and 3 tblsp of the olive oil together. Toss over the fish and leave for 30 minutes.
2. Gently pan-fry the onion in the remaining measure of olive oil until soft but not brown. Stir in the tomato paste and cook, stirring, for 4–5 minutes until it begins to darken in colour. Add the tomatoes and stir well.
3. Drain the fish and discard the marinade. Carefully fold the fish pieces into the hot sauce, simmering very gently for about 5 minutes.
4. Add the chopped oregano, olives and roasted peppers and season with black pepper. Simmer for 1–2 minutes more, until the fish is cooked.

Serves 4–6

smoked fish and potato bake

1 large potato or kumara, peeled
350 grams smoked fish, flaked
1 pepper, diced (optional)
2–3 spring onions, trimmed and finely sliced
2 tblsp chopped fresh parsley
410 gram can **Wattie's Creamy Mushroom Potato Bake Sauce**
pepper to season
¼–½ cup grated cheese
¼–½ cup fresh breadcrumbs

1. Dice the potato or kumara into 1 cm pieces and place in a bowl with the smoked fish, pepper, spring onion, parsley, potato sauce and mix well. Season well with pepper.

2. Turn the mixture into a 4–5-cup-capacity, ovenproof dish and sprinkle over the cheese and breadcrumbs.

3. Bake at 180°C for 1 hour.

4. Serve hot with a salad or try roasted tomatoes to accompany.

Serves **4**

tuna and apple wraps

1 apple, cored and cut into matchsticks or grated
4 spring onions, trimmed and sliced
2–3 tblsp chopped fresh mint
1 yellow pepper, cored and finely sliced
¼ cup finely chopped walnuts
2 cups torn lettuce leaves (or use baby lettuce leaves)
180 gram can **Greenseas Tuna in Springwater**, well drained
¼ cup of your favourite mayonnaise
salt and pepper to season
1 packet (5 plain wraps) Mediterranean-style bread

1 In a bowl mix together the apple, spring onion, mint, pepper, walnuts, lettuce leaves, tuna and mayonnaise. Season with salt and pepper if wished.

2 Take one of the flat bread wraps and place one fifth of the salad mixture in the centre and one end of the bread. Roll up to enclose the filling. Repeat with the remaining ingredients.

3 Cut in half to serve.

Makes 5

tuna pasta bake

4 cups cooked macaroni (or similar shape)
3–4 spring onions, trimmed
2–3 tsp minced garlic
150 gram pouch **Greenseas Tuna Chunks in Springwater**
410 gram can **Wattie's Cheese and Onion Potato Bake Sauce**

topping

2–3 tomatoes, sliced
2–3 tblsp chopped parsley
100 grams crumbled feta or 1 cup grated cheese

1 In a bowl mix together the pasta, onion, garlic, tuna, and potato bake.

2 Turn into a 5–6-cup-capacity ovenproof dish.

3 Bake at 190°C for 30–35 minutes or until hot.

4 Arrange the tomato slices on top and scatter over the parsley and feta or grated cheese. Grill 35 minutes until the cheese browns.

5 Serve immediately with a crisp salad.

Serves 4

frisco grilled fish

4 x 150 gram white fish fillets, skinned
1/2 cup **Eta Mayo Tangy American Style Mayonnaise**
grated rind 1 lemon
1 tbsp fresh lemon juice
2–3 gherkins, very finely chopped
1 tbsp each finely chopped chives and fresh coriander or parsley
1/4 tsp minced chilli paste
1/4 cup dried breadcrumbs
1/2 cup grated cheddar cheese

1. Place the fish on a baking paper-lined tray.
2. Combine the mayonnaise, lemon rind and juice, gherkins, chives, coriander and chilli, and spread evenly over the fish fillets.
3. Mix the breadcrumbs and cheese together and sprinkle on top.
4. Fan grill at 180°C (or grill at 200°C) until the fish is tender and the cheese coating is crisp and golden. Serve with a salad.

Serves 4

warm tuna and noodle salad

dressing
¼ cup lemon juice
¼ cup **Wattie's Bit on the Side Sweet Chilli Sauce**
1 tblsp light soy sauce
1 tblsp honey
2 tblsp sesame seeds, preferably toasted

salad
2 packets **Wattie's Vegetable 99% Fat Free 2 Minute Noodles**
1 tblsp oil
1–2 carrots, peeled and cut into matchsticks
1 bunch broccoli, cut into bite-sized pieces
100–150 grams mushrooms, sliced
150 gram pouch **Greenseas Tuna Chunks in Springwater**
1 cup bean or snowpea sprouts

dressing
1. Put all the dressing ingredients in a screwtop jar and shake well to mix.

salad
1. Pour 4 cups boiling water over the noodles and flavour sachet and stand for 2–3 minutes. Drain well and set aside.
2. Roughly cut the noodles (this makes them easier to toss).
3. Heat the oil in a wok and add the carrots, broccoli and mushrooms and toss quickly until the vegetables are tender but still crisp.
4. Flake in the tuna and add the noodles, bean sprouts and dressing; toss lightly to mix. Serve warm.

Serves 4

thai tuna toss

1–2 tblsp oil (sesame oil is nice here)
1 medium red onion, finely sliced
1 carrot, cut into thin matchsticks
100–150 grams mushrooms, sliced
150 gram pouch **Greenseas Thai Chilli Tuna**
4 tblsp light soy sauce
2 packets **Wattie's Vegetable 99% Fat Free 2 Minute Noodles**
2 tblsp toasted chopped cashew nuts
2 tblsp chopped fresh mint and/or parsley

1. Heat the oil in a frying pan and cook the red onion, carrot and mushrooms over a high heat until lightly cooked.
2. Add the tuna and toss with the soy sauce. Keep warm.
3. Bring 4 cups water to the boil and add the flavour sachet and noodles. Boil for 2–3 minutes before draining.
4. Toss the tuna mix, noodles, cashews, mint and/or parsley together.
5. Serve in deep bowls.

Serves 2

tuna sushi salad

1½ cups short-grain or sushi rice
1½ cups water
¼ cup sushi vinegar
2 tblsp vinegar (use white wine, cider or rice)
2 tblsp oil
¼–½ tsp wasabi (to taste)
150 gram pouch **Greenseas Tuna in Springwater**
1 avocado, peeled, stoned and cubed
½ cucumber, deseeded and finely sliced
pickled ginger to accompany

1. Wash the rice in a sieve until the water runs clear. Drain the rice and stand for 30 minutes.
2. Put the rice and water in a saucepan and bring to the boil. Lower the heat, cover and then simmer for 12 minutes. In the last minute bring the rice back to a boil, before taking off the heat and standing for 15 minutes. Do not remove lid during cooking or standing time.
3. Transfer the rice to a wide container and spread out. Allow to cool for 10 minutes.
4. Mix the sushi vinegar, vinegar, oil and wasabi together and toss through the rice. Flake in the tuna and then gently fold through the avocado and cucumber. Add finely sliced seaweed if wished.
5. Pile into bowls to serve garnished with pickled ginger.

Serves 4

top left warm tuna and noodle salad
middle right thai tuna toss
bottom left tuna sushi salad

parmesan crumbed fish with pesto sauce

1 egg
¼ cup milk
½ cup fresh or dry breadcrumbs
½ cup finely grated parmesan cheese
4 fillets of firm white fish
¼ cup seasoned flour
3–4 tblsp oil or butter for frying
2 courgettes, thickly sliced
400 gram can **Wattie's Pesto Style Tomatoes**

1. Beat the egg and milk together. Mix the breadcrumbs and cheese together. Coat the fish fillets in the seasoned flour, shaking off the excess.
2. Dip the fish into the egg mix and then coat in the breadcrumbs. Refrigerate.
3. Heat the oil or butter in a frying pan and cook the courgettes until they are golden and tender. Set aside and keep warm.
4. Add the fish to the hot pan and cook for 2–3 minutes each side until the fish flakes easily.
5. Heat the pesto tomatoes.
6. Serve the fish on the courgette slices with a spoonful of hot pesto tomatoes to accompany. If wished, garnish with shavings of parmesan and a few leaves of fresh herbs.

Serves 4

vegetarian

{vegetarian} tips and hints

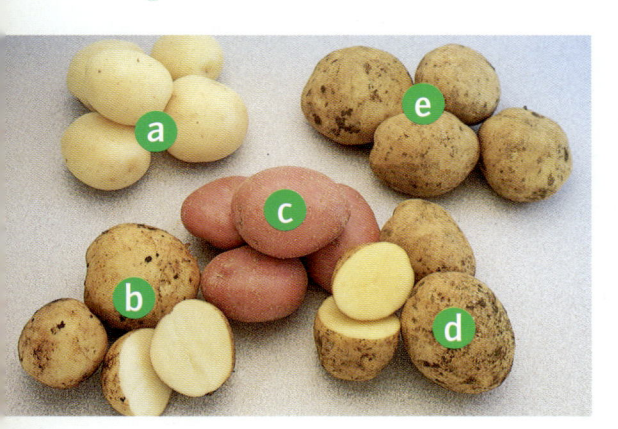

1 When buying potatoes, we can choose between floury, waxy or all-purpose potatoes.

Waxy potatoes are early-season potatoes and they are waxy because their sugar has not yet converted to starch as it will with age. They are best suited for boiling, salads and casseroles.
Varieties — Draga, Frisia, Jersey Bennie, Nadine (a)

Floury potatoes are low in moisture and sugar and high in starch, making them perfect for mashing, baking, roasting, chips, or pureed soups.
Varieties — Ilam Hardy (b), Russet Burbank, Red Rascal (c), Agria (d), Fianna, White Delight

All-purpose potatoes have been bred for a wide range of cooking styles.
Varieties — Delcora, Desiree, Karaka, Rocket, Rua (e), Stroma

2 Do not keep potatoes in the fridge, but rather a well-ventilated area in a cool dark place. Always remove from the plastic bag as they will sweat and develop a greening under the skin. New potatoes are more susceptible to greening than old ones.

3 Wattie's Freshlock™ frozen vegetables are snap-frozen soon after picking to keep their nutritional content. As they have been blanched there is no need to overcook; rather reheat them in a minimal amount of water. Cooking in lots of water will make them soggy and leach out their valuable nutritional content.

4 The heat in chillies is contained in the sack that surrounds the seeds. Try to cut the chilli seeds out with a small knife otherwise if you use your hands, wash them well afterwards.

5 Keep brown, white or red onions in a cool dry place. Do not store in a plastic bag as this causes condensation and then decay. Red onions are sweeter and juicer than other varieties and are excellent for eating raw in salad. They do not keep as well as red or white. If you only use half an onion, keep the other half well wrapped and in a container in the fridge as it will taint foods, such as dairy foods. Should the container be tainted with onion, rinse with a little vanilla essence.

6 When cooking with filo pastry, work with one sheet at a time, keeping the remaining sheets under a lightly damp cloth. Filo sheets will dry out quickly if left uncovered and they will become brittle and break when you go to roll them.

7 When buying asparagus, look for tightly furled tips. The stems should be straight, not droopy, which indicates they are old and not worth having. Wrap the end of the bundle in damp, absorbent paper and keep in the vegetable drawer of the refrigerator.

8 When using celery, do not forget to use the leaves, chopped up and added at the last minute. They have great celery flavour. If your celery becomes limp, trim the end off and stand in a jar of cold water. The celery will drink the water and become crisp.

9 When cooking Brussels sprouts, peel away the coarse, outer leaves and then cut a cross in the base of the sprout. This ensures the inside cooks at the same time as the outer leaves.

10 Be experimental with grains and pulses. Adding them to curries and casseroles will increase texture and fibre. They can be purchased dry, or canned and ready to use. If you buy them dry, replace them regularly. Once they become old (6 months), they can take longer to cook and often remain tough.

tomato, basil and mozzarella pizza

2 prepared thin pizza bases
1 cup **Wattie's Italian Seasoned Tomatoes**
1 cup fresh basil leaves, torn
1 red onion, sliced
¼ cup kalamata olives
200 gram fresh mozzarella or grated pizza cheese
salt and pepper to season

1. Place the pizza bases on a greased tray and spread with the seasoned tomatoes. Sprinkle with basil leaves.
2. Pan-fry the onion slices until starting to brown. Arrange on the bases with the olives.
3. Sprinkle the cheese evenly on both pizzas and season with salt and pepper.
4. Bake at 200°C for 15–20 minutes.

Makes 2 pizzas

cheese and walnut potato slice

410 gram can **Wattie's Cheese and Onion Potato Bake Sauce**
3 eggs
1 tblsp butter, melted
1 tsp minced fresh garlic
1 kg potatoes, peeled and thinly sliced
1 red pepper, diced
3 spring onions, trimmed and finely chopped
¼ cup chopped walnuts
½ cup grated smoked cheese

1. Beat together the potato bake and eggs. Butter the inside of a 6-cup-capacity ovenproof dish and scatter over the garlic.
2. Spread half the potato bake sauce and egg mixture over the dish. Layer half the potatoes, red pepper and spring onion in the dish, top with half the potato bake and then repeat the layers. Sprinkle over nuts and cheese.
3. Bake at 180°C for 50–60 minutes until the potatoes are tender. Cool and serve cut in wedges.

Serves 4–6

green thai vegetable curry

1 tblsp oil
1 large onion, diced
2 tsp minced garlic
2 tblsp green Thai curry paste*
400 gram can coconut cream or milk
250 grams pumpkin, peeled and diced

250 grams potatoes, peeled and diced
2 green peppers, diced
2 cups frozen **Wattie's Freshlock™ Baby Green Beans**
2 tblsp fish sauce
2 tsp brown sugar
2 tblsp chopped fresh coriander

1 Heat the oil in a medium-sized saucepan and pan-fry the onion for 1–2 minutes. Add the garlic and curry paste and cook for 2 minutes.

2 Add the coconut cream or milk, pumpkin, potatoes and peppers. Cover and simmer for 20 minutes or until the vegetables are tender.

3 Add the beans and fish sauce, cover and simmer for a further 5 minutes.

4 Stir in the brown sugar and coriander.

5 Serve over steamed rice, garnished with cashew nuts if wished.

Serves 4

*Use any prepared store-purchased green Thai curry paste.

black-eyed bean casserole

4 tblsp oil
2 tsp cumin seeds (or use 2 tsp ground)
1 cinnamon stick (or use ½ tsp cinnamon)
2 tsp ground coriander
½ tsp each of cayenne and turmeric
1 onion, peeled and finely chopped
4 tsp minced garlic
250 grams mushrooms, sliced
425 gram can black-eyed beans, well drained
250 grams pumpkin, diced
1½ cups vegetable stock or water
400 gram can **Wattie's Whole Peeled Tomatoes in Juice**
salt and pepper
2 tblsp chopped fresh oregano (optional)

1. Heat the oil in a large lidded frying pan or large saucepan. Add the spices, onion and garlic and cook over a moderate heat until the onion has softened.
2. Add the mushrooms, beans, pumpkin, stock or water, tomatoes and juice.
3. Simmer gently over a moderate heat for about 25–30 minutes until the pumpkin is tender.
4. Season with salt and pepper and add the oregano if using.

Serves 4

spinach and feta filo pie

1 tblsp oil
2 onions, peeled and finely sliced
500 grams frozen **Wattie's Freshlock™ Chopped Spinach**, defrosted
2 x 250 gram tubs Tararua Cottage Cheese
200 grams feta cheese, crumbled
3 tblsp chopped fresh oregano, marjoram or mint
salt and pepper to season
4 tblsp butter, melted
16 sheets filo pastry
1–2 tblsp sesame seeds (optional)

1. Heat the oil in a frying pan and cook the onion for 3–5 minutes until tender. Cool.
2. Squeeze the spinach very firmly between two plates to drain off excess water. Mix together the spinach, cottage cheese, feta cheese, onion and herbs. Season.
3. Butter 8 filo sheets and line a 2 cm-deep pie dish. Spoon the spinach filling in evenly. Fold over the filo edges. Brush the remaining filo sheets with butter and arrange on top. Sprinkle with sesame seeds if wished.
4. Bake at 190°C (fan-bake 170°C) for 35–40 minutes.

Serves 6

variation
- Make 3–4 dents in the spinach filling and place a cracked egg in each.

roast pumpkin, cashew nut burgers

500 grams pumpkin, peeled and cut into large pieces
3 tblsp oil
salt and pepper to season
300 gram can **Craig's Chickpeas in Brine**, well drained
½ cup toasted cashew nuts

1 egg
¼ cup chopped fresh parsley
½ red onion, finely diced
½ cup dry breadcrumbs
flour

1. Toss the pumpkin in 1 tablespoon of the oil. Season well with salt and pepper. Roast at 180°C for 30–35 minutes until cooked. Cool.

2. In a food processor put the pumpkin, chickpeas, cashew nuts, egg, parsley, red onion and breadcrumbs. Pulse until well mixed. If too wet add more breadcrumbs.

3. Shape into 6 patties with floured hands. Pan-fry in the remaining oil for 2–3 minutes on each side until hot and golden.

4. Serve with your favourite salad.

Serves 6

parsnip bake

2 large parsnips
25 grams butter
1/2 cup cream
salt and pepper to season
1–2 tblsp oil
2 small leeks, trimmed and finely sliced
2 tsp minced garlic
425 gram can aduki beans
1 cup **Wattie's Tomato Purée**
2 tblsp chopped parsley
1 tsp soy sauce
1 tsp each of caraway seeds and ground allspice
1 cup grated cheese
chives to garnish

1. Peel and cook the parsnips in boiling water. Drain. Mash with the butter and cream. Season with salt and pepper.
2. Heat the oil in a large frying pan and cook the leeks and garlic for 5 minutes.
3. Mix together the beans, tomato purée, parsley, soy sauce, caraway seeds and allspice.
4. In a casserole spread half the parsnip purée, top with the leeks, then the bean mixture and finish with the remaining parsnip.
5. Sprinkle with the cheese. Bake at 180°C for 40 minutes or until piping hot. Garnish with chives.

Serves 4–6

tandoori tofu kebabs with kashmir rice

tofu
5 tblsp tandoori spice mix
6 tblsp water
500 grams firm tofu, cut into 3 cm dice
2 cups fine fresh breadcrumbs
oil for shallow frying

rice
2 tblsp oil
1 onion, peeled and finely diced
1 tblsp minced ginger
1 tblsp curry powder
1 cup long-grain rice (try Basmati)
1 1/2 cups water
1/2 cup raisins
1/2 cup toasted cashew nuts
1/4 cup chopped fresh coriander or parsley
425 gram can **Wattie's Mango Slices in Syrup**, well drained and sliced

sauce
400 gram can **Wattie's Indian Spiced Tomatoes**
1/2 cup yoghurt, coconut cream or cream (optional)
2 tblsp chopped fresh coriander or parsley

tofu
1. Stir the tandoori mix and water together and pour over the tofu. Toss to coat.
2. Toss the tofu in the breadcrumbs. Heat the oil until it is hot enough to shallow-fry — 180°C. Cook the tofu until golden and then place on absorbent paper to drain. Serve, skewered if wished, over the rice with the sauce and slices of mango.

rice
1. Heat the oil in a saucepan and cook the onion and ginger until it is soft. Add the spices and cook for a further minute.
2. Stir in the rice and water and bring to the boil. Lower the heat, cover and simmer gently for 12 minutes. Turn off the heat and allow to stand for 5 more minutes. Stir in the raisins, cashews and coriander or parsley. Season if wished.

sauce
1. Purée the Indian tomatoes and then place in a saucepan. Stir over a low heat until hot. Add the yoghurt, coconut cream or cream if using and the coriander or parsley.

Serves 4–6

potato and parmesan cakes with tuscan sauce

700 grams potatoes, skin on (or 4 medium-sized)
½ cup grated parmesan cheese
½ cup basil leaves, sliced
2–3 spring onions, trimmed and sliced
¼ cup pinenuts or pistachio nuts
1 egg

salt and pepper to season
3 tblsp butter
3 tblsp oil
400 gram pouch **Wattie's Simply Cuisine Tuscan Pasta Sauce**

1. Scrub the potatoes and place in a saucepan, cover with water and bring to the boil. Cook for 10–12 minutes until still firm inside when tested with a small knife. Strain and cool for 10 minutes.
2. Peel the potato skin off. Working quickly to keep the potato warm, coarsely grate it and put in a bowl with the parmesan, basil, spring onion, pinenuts and egg. Season with salt and pepper and mix together. With your hands, shape into 8 small cakes.
3. Heat the butter and oil in a frying pan until quite hot. Fry the potato cakes 3–4 at a time until crispy on both sides.
4. Heat the sauce while cooking the potato cakes. Serve the potato cakes hot with plenty of sauce, garnished with freshly shaved parmesan and basil leaves if wished.

Makes 8 Serves 4 as a light meal

indian potato and tomato curry

1 tblsp oil
1 tblsp each of mustard seeds, coriander seeds and cumin seeds
2 x 400 gram cans **Wattie's Indian Spiced Tomatoes**
1 cup red lentils, washed and strained
3 cups water
1 tsp salt
500 grams potatoes, peeled and diced into 2 cm pieces
1 tblsp garam masala
2 tblsp chopped fresh mint or coriander
steamed rice to accompany

1 Heat the oil in a saucepan and add the spices, stirring for 1–2 minutes. When the mustard seeds begin to pop, pour in the tomatoes.

2 Add the red lentils, water and salt and stir to mix. Cover and allow to simmer for 10–15 minutes until the lentils are nearly cooked.

3 Add the diced potatoes and continue to cook, covered, for 10–15 minutes until the potatoes are tender.

4 Serve on rice if wished, sprinkled with garam masala and chopped fresh mint or coriander to garnish.

Serves 6

Note: You could serve the curry as part of an Indian meal with Butter Chicken (page 79) or Rogan Josh (page 112).

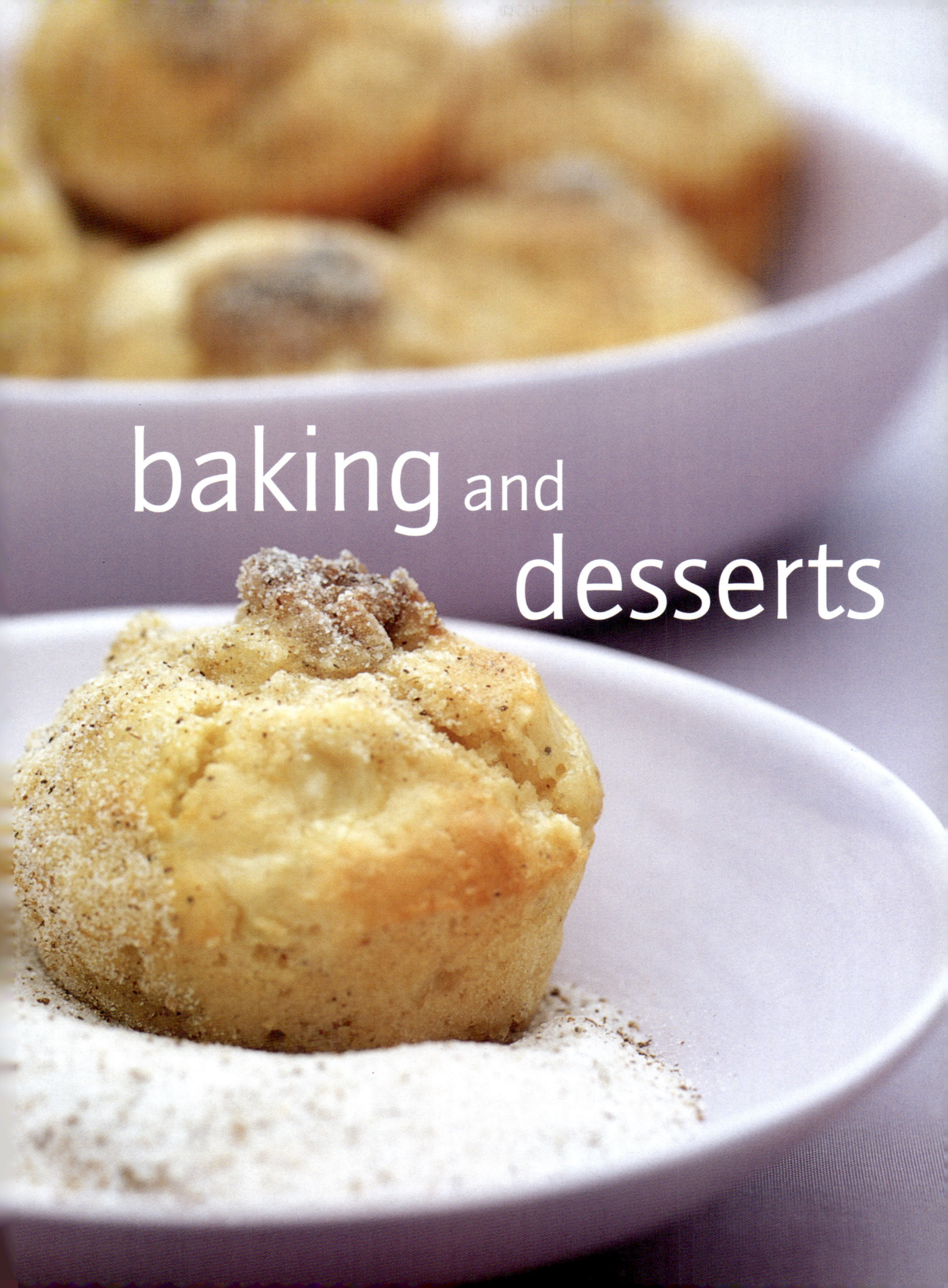

baking and desserts

{baking and desserts}
tips and hints

1 If self-raising flour is kept too long and becomes stale or old it can lose its ability to rise properly. Buy as required and use soon after purchase. The same applies to baking powder: keep it turned over regularly.

2 Vanilla essence is available as pure and imitation. Pure vanilla essence is the best vanilla essence to buy as it has a softer, stronger flavour, whereas imitation vanilla essence is harsh. I use imitation essence to wipe out the fridge with, to give it a fresh smell, or wipe over tupperware, when it has become tainted with food odours.

3 Although ordinary sugar is perfectly acceptable for most styles of bakery, castor sugar will give a lighter result, especially for sponges.

4 Desiccated coconut has a high oil content and should be kept in the freezer to prevent it from going rancid.

5 If you mix cakes in a food processor, begin by processing the eggs and sugar together first, and then add the softened butter. This prevents a solid layer of butter and sugar from forming under the blade and ensures a softly processed mass. As no air is being incorporated, do not expect the mixture to be as light and fluffy as that mixed with beaters.

6. Do not keep cakes and biscuits in the same tin. Soft baking such as cakes and loaves will cause crisp baking like biscuits and slices to soften. Keep them in separate and airtight containers.

7. When baking have the butter and eggs at room temperature to ensure they beat together successfully. If they cannot be left out of the refrigerator, soften the butter in the microwave, but DO NOT melt it. This turns the butter into an oil and once this happens it cannot be used to cream with the sugar and eggs. Begin again.

8. Store chocolate tightly wrapped in a cool, dry place, not the refrigerator, as chocolate will absorb other odours. Too warm a temperature will cause a 'bloom' or a mottled or streaked surface to occur: this is the cocoa butter rising to the top. It will not affect the chocolate.

9. If you are adding honey or golden syrup to a recipe, either warm the spoon or rub the spoon with oil before dipping it into the honey or golden syrup, which will then fall easily off the spoon.

10. Muffins and scones need a very light hand to mix. If you over-beat muffins they will peak like Mt Everest when they cook. Fold by lifting a slotted spoon through from the edge of the bowl into the centre and then turning the batter over. Turn the bowl regularly.

orange and mango cheesecake ice cream

2 x 250 gram tubs cream cheese
grated rind and juice 2 oranges
425 gram can **Wattie's Mangoes in Syrup**, well drained
2 eggs
2 egg yolks
¾ cup castor sugar

1. Process the cream cheese, orange rind and juice and mangoes in a food processor until the cream cheese is very smooth and the mangoes puréed.
2. In a clean bowl mix together the eggs, egg yolks and castor sugar until the mixture is very thick and pale lemon in colour.
3. Add the egg mixture to the cream mixture and pulse to combine. Alternatively, fold together with a holed spoon.
4. Pour into a wide, plastic wrap-lined, 6-cup-capacity loaf tin. Cover with foil and freeze overnight or until solid.
5. Serve in scoops or slices with tropical fruit salad or fresh fruits.

Serves 6–8

no-fuss apple tart

250 grams very soft butter (but not melted)
¾ cup castor sugar
1 egg
grated rind 1 orange
1 tsp vanilla essence
2½ cups self-raising flour
400 gram can **Wattie's Simply Apple Dices**

1. In a bowl or food processor beat together the butter, castor sugar, egg, orange rind and vanilla essence until creamy and well mixed.
2. Stir or pulse in the self-raising flour.
3. Spread two thirds of the mixture into the base of a well greased and floured 23 cm, loose-bottom cake tin. Spread over the apple.
4. Dot the remaining dough over the top.
5. Bake at 190°C for 40 minutes. When cool dust with icing sugar and serve with lashings of whipped cream.

Serves 6–8

peach and cream cheese slice

100 grams softened butter
¾ cup sugar
2 eggs
1½ cups self-raising flour
½ cup desiccated coconut
¼ cup milk

topping
820 gram can **Wattie's Peach Slices in Syrup**, well drained
250 gram tub cream cheese
¼ cup sugar
1 egg
dash vanilla essence (optional)
ground cinnamon

1. Put the butter, sugar, eggs, flour, coconut and milk into a food processor and process only until blended.
2. Spread into a greased and lined, 24 cm x 30 cm slice tin.
3. Arrange the peach slices randomly or in neat, even rows on top.
4. Blend the cream cheese, sugar, egg and vanilla essence, if used, together in the food processor and pour over the top.
5. Bake at 190°C for 20–25 minutes until golden and well risen.
6. Serve hot or cold in wedges with whipped cream and dusted with ground cinnamon.

Serves 6–8

fruity blueberry self-saucing pudding

pudding
2 cups self-raising flour
¼ cup sugar
100 grams butter
1 egg
1 cup milk
grated rind 1 lemon
1½ cups frozen blueberries

sauce
375 gram jar **Craig's Blueberry Jam**
1 cup boiling water

1. Sift the flour and sugar into a bowl. Rub in the butter until the mixture forms coarse crumbs.
2. Blend the egg, milk and lemon rind together and pour into the dry ingredients. Mix together gently.
3. Scatter the blueberries over the base of a well-greased, 2-litre-capacity pie dish. Dot the batter on top.
4. Mix the jam with the hot water and pour carefully over the top of the batter.
5. Bake at 180°C for 40–45 minutes until the pudding is golden and well risen.
6. Stand for 5 minutes before serving with whipped cream as the sauce is very hot.

Serves 4–6

easy apricot and ginger mousse

12 ginger crunch biscuits*
410 gram can **Wattie's Apricot Pieces in Syrup**, well drained
1 cup apricot yoghurt
grated rind and juice 1 orange
1 cup cream

1. Place the biscuits in a food processor and process to a fine crumb. Set aside.
2. Place three quarters of the apricots in the food processor with the apricot yoghurt and the orange rind and juice. Process until smooth.
3. In a clean bowl, lightly whip the cream. Add the puréed mixture and fold together.
4. In 4 individual glasses spread a layer of the apricot mousse. Sprinkle over a tablespoon of the crushed biscuits, and repeat with a further layer of both, then top with a finishing layer of mousse.
5. Slice the remaining apricots and arrange on top with the grated orange rind to garnish. Refrigerate for 30 minutes before serving.

Serves 4

Use ginger crunch not ginger nut biscuits which are too hard for this recipe.

sour cream apple pie

2 cups flour
½ tsp baking powder
¼ cup sugar
175 grams chilled butter
2–3 tblsp water
800 gram can **Wattie's Simply Apple Slices**
½ cup sour cream
1 egg
grated rind 1 lemon

1. Put the flour, baking powder, sugar and butter into a food processor and process until the mixture resembles fine crumbs. Pour sufficient water down the feed tube and pulse until the mixture resembles small, moist balls of dough.
2. Turn out and bring together. Roll out to a 30 cm round and place over the base and sides of a 24 cm flan tin.
3. In a bowl mix together the apple, sour cream, egg and lemon rind and pour into the centre of the pastry-lined tin. Flip the edges over.
4. Bake at 190°C for 35–40 minutes.

Serves 6–8

fruity blueberry self-saucing pudding

peach cake

175 grams butter, softened
1 cup castor sugar
3 eggs
grated rind 2 lemons or oranges
2 cups self-raising flour
¼ cup custard powder
410 gram can **Wattie's Peach Slices in Syrup**, well drained

icing

2½ cups icing sugar, sifted
¼ cup lemon or orange juice

1. Beat the butter, sugar, eggs and lemon or orange rind together until light and fluffy. Mix in the sifted flour and custard powder.
2. Spread two thirds of the mixture into a 22–23 cm-round, greased and baking paper-lined cake tin.
3. Scatter the peaches on top. Spread the remaining cake batter on top.
4. Bake at 180°C for 45–50 minutes until well risen and golden. Cool in the tin before icing.

icing

1. Mix together icing sugar and lemon or orange juice.

Makes 1 cake

baked jam roll

125 grams softened butter
2 cups self-raising flour
¾–1 cup milk
about ½ cup **Craig's Apricot Jam**

syrup

¾ cup sugar
50 grams melted butter
1 cup boiling water

1. Rub the butter into the flour until the mixture resembles fine crumbs. Add sufficient milk to make a medium-firm dough. Turn out onto a lightly floured board and bring together.
2. Roll out to 1 cm thickness. Spread with the apricot jam, leaving a 1 cm free edge. Roll up like a Swiss roll and place in a greased, ovenproof dish.
3. Make the syrup by stirring together the sugar, butter and boiling water. Pour over the roll.
4. Bake at 180°C for about 45 minutes until the roll is golden and well risen. Serve sliced with a little of the self-saucing sauce and custard or cream.

Serves 6

creamy plum tart

pastry
1¼ cups flour
1 tsp baking powder
2 tblsp sugar
100 grams butter
3–4 tblsp milk

filling
250 gram tub sour cream
2 eggs
2 tblsp castor sugar
½ tsp vanilla essence
½ 850 gram can **Wattie's Black Doris Plums in Syrup**, halved and stoned
ground cinnamon or allspice
icing sugar or castor sugar for dusting

pastry
1. Put the flour, baking powder and sugar into a food processor and pulse to sift.
2. Add the butter and process until it resembles coarse crumbs. Pulse in sufficient milk to form a dough.
3. Turn onto a board and knead lightly. Wrap and chill for 30 minutes. Roll the pastry out to line the base and sides of a 20 cm loose-bottom flan dish, preferably metal.

filling
1. Beat the sour cream, eggs, sugar and vanilla essence together. Pour into the pastry-lined flan.
2. Arrange the plums cut side up in the filling. Sprinkle with cinnamon or allspice.
3. Bake at 180°C for 50 minutes. Dust with icing sugar or castor sugar before serving.

Serves 6–8

eccles cakes

2 packets pre-rolled frozen puff pastry sheets, defrosted
400 gram can **Wattie's Simply Apple Dices**
400 gram pottle Christmas fruit mince

glaze
1 egg, beaten, to glaze
about 2 tblsp castor sugar

1. Cut 9–10 cm rounds from each sheet of pastry. Layer and re-roll the scraps.
2. Mix the apple and fruit mince together and place in the centre of the pastry round. Bring the outside edges up to enclose. Pinch to seal.
3. Turn over so the join is underneath and roll the balls out with a rolling pin until the fruit mince can just be seen under the pastry.
4. Make three shallow cuts in the top layer of pastry. Brush with beaten egg to glaze and sprinkle each with a little castor sugar.
5. Bake on a greased tray at 220°C for 12–15 minutes until golden and cooked. Serve warm, dusted with icing sugar, ice cream and whipped cream or simply dusted with icing sugar and served warm with coffee.

Makes 48

maiden tarts

400 gram block frozen sweet pastry, defrosted
about ½ cup **Craig's Jam** (any flavour)
100 grams softened butter
½ cup sugar
1 tsp vanilla essence
1 egg
1 cup self-raising flour (or use ½ ground almonds and ½ self-raising flour)
¼ cup milk
icing sugar for dusting

1. Roll the pastry out onto a floured board to 3–4 mm thickness. Cut out 7 cm rounds and use to line 18 tartlet moulds. Fill each with ½ tsp jam.
2. Beat the butter and sugar together until creamy and then beat in the vanilla essence and egg. Fold in the sifted flour and milk.
3. Place about 1 tblsp of mixture on top of the jam tarts. Use any remaining pastry scraps to make a thin cross on top.
4. Bake at 180°C for 18–20 minutes until well risen and golden.
5. Serve dusted with icing sugar.

Makes 18

creamy jam tarts

400 gram block frozen sweet pastry, defrosted
your favourite **Craig's Jam** for the filling
1 tsp ground instant coffee granules
1 tblsp hot water
1 cup cream
icing sugar to sweeten
cocoa for dusting

1. Roll the pastry out on a floured board to 3–4 mm thickness. Cut out 8 cm rounds and use to line 16–18 tartlet moulds. Use any remaining pieces to make 16–18 thick stems about 2 cm long.
2. Bake the tartlets blind at 200°C for 10–12 minutes until cooked. Remove the baking blind material. Bake the stems at the same time.
3. Place a teaspoon of your favourite jam in the centre of each tart.
4. Dissolve the coffee in the hot water and cool. Whip the cream and coffee lightly and sweeten to taste with icing sugar. Top with a little whipped cream and place a stem in the centre of each tart. Dust with cocoa to serve.

Makes 16–18

top maiden tarts   **middle** eccles cakes   **bottom** creamy jam tarts

strawberry meringues

meringue
3 egg whites
1 1/4 cups icing sugar, sifted
1/4 cup flaked almonds

strawberry filling
1 punnet strawberries, hulled
2 tblsp orange juice
1/2 cup **Craig's Strawberry Jam**
whipped cream to accompany

meringue

1. Place the egg whites and half the icing sugar in a clean bowl and beat on high speed for about 4–5 minutes until the mixture is thick and glossy. **(a)**
2. Add the remaining icing sugar and continue beating until the mixture is very thick and has a strong sheen. **(b)**
3. Spread about 2 tablespoonfuls of the mixture into 24 x 7 cm rounds, onto baking paper-lined baking trays. **(c)** Sprinkle one third of the meringues with the flaked almonds.
4. Cook at 120°C for 1 1/2 hours or until well dried out. They should be just off-white in colour. Cool on the trays until cold and then store in an airtight container.
5. Layer the meringues with the Strawberry Filling and whipped cream. **(d)**

strawberry filling

1. Purée a quarter of the strawberries with the orange juice. Quarter the remaining strawberries and toss with the purée and jam.

Serves **8**

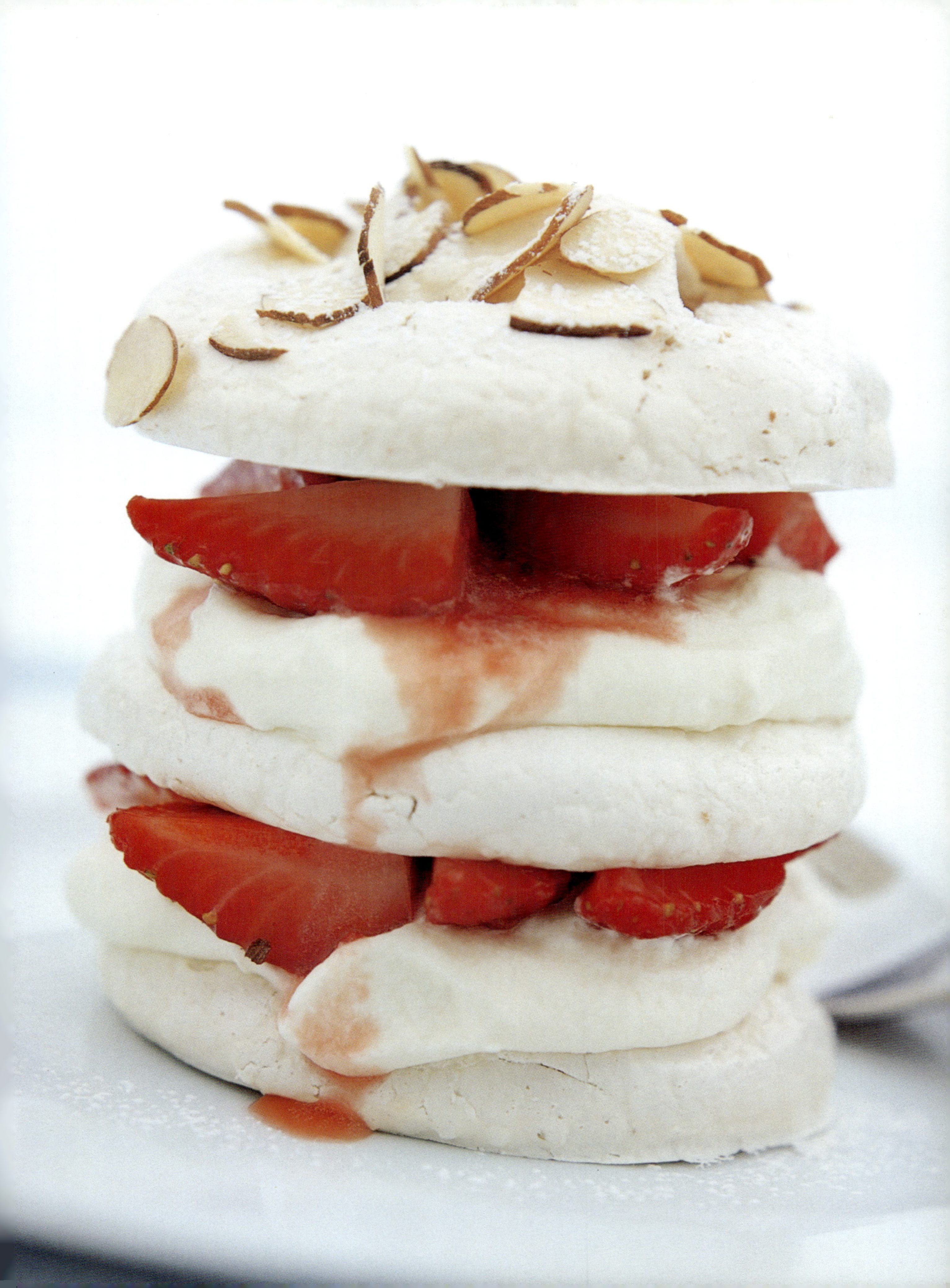

nutty banoffie pie

2 sheets defrosted, pre-rolled sweet short pastry
75 grams butter
1/2 cup firmly packed brown sugar
250 gram tub **Mainland Traditional Cream Cheese**
1/2 – 3/4 cup **Eta Smooth Peanut Butter**
1 egg
3 bananas, peeled

topping (optional)
whipped cream
grated chocolate

1. Roll the 2 sheets of short pastry together until they are large enough to line the base and sides of a 24 cm, loose-bottom flan tin. Trim the edges.
2. Line the pastry with baking paper and fill with baking blind material.
3. Bake at 190°C for 12 minutes, and then remove the baking blind material and return the flan to the oven for a further 5–7 minutes until the pastry is well cooked. Cool.
4. Put the butter and sugar in a saucepan and when the butter has melted, simmer for 1 minute.
5. Stir in the cream cheese and peanut butter and continue to stir until the mixture is smooth and thick. Quickly beat in the egg. Remove from the heat.
6. Slice the bananas over the base of the pastry flan, then pour over the peanut toffee filling. Refrigerate for 2 hours or until required. Serve plain or topped with whipped cream. If wished, garnish with grated chocolate.

Serves 8–10

boysenberry ripple cake with custard

cake

125 grams butter, softened
1 cup castor sugar
1 egg
1½ cups self-raising flour
2 tsp ground cinnamon
1 tsp mixed spice
¼ tsp salt
430 gram can **Wattie's Boysenberries in Syrup**, well drained
½ cup milk

topping

½ cup brown sugar
25 grams butter, melted
½ cup rolled oats
1 tsp mixed spice

cake

1. Beat the butter and sugar together until light and creamy. Add the egg and beat well.
2. Sift the flour, cinnamon, mixed spice and salt together and fold into the creamed mixture with the boysenberries and milk.
3. Turn into a lightly greased and floured, 20 cm cake tin.
4. Sprinkle over the topping.
5. Bake at 180°C for 40–45 minutes until cooked when tested with a skewer. Cool on a cake rack and serve with warm custard.

topping

1. Mix together the brown sugar, melted butter, rolled oats and spice.

apple muffins with spicy topping

muffins

- 3 cups flour
- 2 tblsp baking powder
- ¾ cup castor sugar
- 1 tsp each ground ginger and mixed spice
- 2 eggs
- 400 gram can **Wattie's Simply Apple Dices**
- 1½ cups milk
- few drops vanilla essence
- 100 grams melted butter, cooled
- 16 walnut halves (optional)

topping

- 2–3 tblsp butter, melted
- 1 tsp each castor sugar and mixed spice, mixed together

muffins

1. Sift the flour, baking powder, castor sugar and spices into a bowl.
2. Mix together the eggs, apple, milk and vanilla essence. Make a well in the centre of the bowl and pour in the apple and milk mixture. Stir gently with a holed spoon until the batter is just mixed. Fold through the butter.
3. Do not over-mix the batter mixture as the muffins will peak like Mt Everest. Lift the mixture up with the spoon and turn it over on top of the remaining mix in the bowl. Give the bowl a quarter turn and then repeat this lifting and mixing routine until all ingredients are just blended.
4. Three-quarters fill 16 well-greased muffin tins. Decorate each muffin with a walnut half, if using.
5. Bake at 220°C for about 15–20 minutes until well risen, golden and cooked.

topping

1. Remove from the oven and wait for 2–3 minutes. Brush the tops of the muffins with the melted butter and sprinkle over the mixed spice sugar.

Makes 16

peanut slice

- 200 grams softened butter
- 1 cup sugar
- 1 egg
- 2 cups flour
- ½ tsp baking powder
- 397 gram can sweetened condensed milk
- 2 tblsp golden syrup
- 375 gram jar **Eta Smooth** or **Crunchy Peanut Butter**

1. Beat the butter and sugar together until the mixture is pale in colour and light in texture. Add the egg and beat well.
2. Sift in the flour and baking powder and mix to form a soft dough. Press three quarters of the dough onto the base of a baking paper-lined, 20 cm x 30 cm slice tin.
3. In a saucepan warm the condensed milk and golden syrup. Stir in the peanut butter. Spread evenly over the base of the slice. Dot the remaining dough over the top of the peanut layer.
4. Bake at 180°C for 30–35 minutes until the slice is golden. Cool in the tin before cutting into slices to serve. Keep in an airtight container.

Makes 30 pieces

louise cake

- 100 grams butter, softened
- ¼ cup castor sugar
- 3 eggs, separated
- 1 tsp vanilla essence
- 2 tblsp milk
- 2 cups self-raising flour
- ½ cup any Craig's red jam (raspberry, plum or currant)
- ¾ cup castor sugar
- ¾ cup coconut

1. Put the butter, first measure of castor sugar, egg yolks and vanilla essence into a food processor and process until well mixed.
2. Add the milk and flour and process only until combined.
3. Spread the mixture into a greased and lined, 24 cm x 30 cm slice tin. Spread with the red jam.
4. In a clean bowl whisk the egg whites until stiff but not dry. Add the second measure of castor sugar and beat until thick. Fold in the coconut. Spread over the slice.
5. Bake at 180°C for 25–30 minutes. Cool and slice into squares.

Makes 30 pieces

apple muffins with spicy topping

creamy tropical muffins

2 cups flour
1 tsp baking soda
2 tsp baking powder
½ cup sugar
1 cup bran
425 gram can **Wattie's Tropical Fruit Salad Chunks**
1 egg
¾ cup fruit salad yoghurt
100 grams butter, melted
about ½ cup cream cheese

1. Sift the flour, baking soda, baking powder and sugar into a bowl. Stir in the bran.
2. Roughly chop the fruit chunks with juice, egg and fruit salad yoghurt in a food processor. Pour into the dry ingredients and fold together with the butter.
3. Half-fill 12 well-greased muffin tins. Place a teaspoon of cream cheese in the centre of each and top with the remaining muffin mixture.
4. Bake at 220°C for 15–18 minutes until cooked.

Makes 12

chocolate berry cheesecake

250 grams sweet plain chocolate biscuits
100 grams butter, melted
430 gram can **Wattie's Boysenberries**
500 gram tub Tararua Cheesecake Mix
2 tsp gelatin

1. Crush the biscuits in a food processor or by placing in a sealed plastic bag and crushing with a rolling pin. Stir in the melted butter. Press into the base and sides of a 23cm loose bottom flan tin. Refrigerate until required.
2. Drain and reserve the juice from the boysenberries.
3. Beat together the drained boysenberries and cheesecake mix until smooth. Spread into the prepared flan. Refrigerate for 1 hour before serving like this, or if you like, top with the boysenberry glaze.
4. Sprinkle the gelatin over the reserved boysenberry juice and when it has been absorbed, warm in the microwave for 2 minutes on high and stir until dissolved. Cool. Pour over the chilled cheesecake and refrigerate a further hour before serving.

Serves 6

apple and date loaf

1 cup chopped dried dates
1 tsp baking soda
400 gram can **Wattie's Simply Apple Dices**
2 tblsp finely chopped crystallised ginger
2 tsp ground ginger

¼ cup boiling water
2 tblsp softened butter
¾ cup sugar (castor is best)
1 egg
2 cups self-raising flour, sifted

1. In a bowl put the dates, baking soda, apple, crystallised ginger, ground ginger and boiling water and stir well.
2. In another bowl mix the butter and sugar together and then beat in the egg. Gradually blend in the date mixture and sifted flour.
3. Spoon into a greased, floured and lined 25 cm x 11 cm x 7 cm loaf tin.
4. Bake at 180°C for 1 hour or until the loaf is cooked when tested with a skewer. Cool in the tin for 10 minutes before turning out onto a cake rack to cool. Serve sliced with butter or a slice of cheddar cheese for a change.

Makes **1** loaf

variations
- Use New Zealand dried apricots instead of dates.
- Use mixed peel instead of crystallised ginger and replace the ground ginger with mixed spice or ground cardamom.
- Use brown sugar instead of white sugar.

blueberry chocolate cake

½ cup cocoa
¾ cup hot water
250 grams butter, softened
1 cup brown sugar
1 tsp vanilla essence

3 eggs
375 gram jar **Craig's Blueberry Jam**
2½ cups self-raising flour
grated chocolate for decoration (optional)

1. Stir the cocoa and hot water together until smooth. Cool thoroughly.
2. Beat the butter, brown sugar and vanilla essence together until light and fluffy. Beat in the eggs one at a time, beating well after each addition. Beat in ½ cup of the jam.
3. Sift in the self-raising flour and pour in the cooled chocolate mixture. Fold together carefully. Spread into a well-greased and floured, 22 cm–23 cm ring cake tin.
4. Bake at 180°C for 40 minutes or until a skewer inserted comes out clean and the cake has shrunk from the sides of the cake tin. Cool in the cake tin for 5 minutes before turning out on to a cake rack to cool.
5. When cool, split the cake in half or three layers horizontally and spread the cut layers with the remaining jam. Join together. Dust with icing sugar or spread with Thick Chocolate Glaze and a little grated chocolate for decoration.

thick chocolate glaze

1. Microwave 125 grams chocolate chips and ¼ cup cream (plain or sour) in a microwave-proof jug for 1 minute on high power. Stir until the chocolate has all melted and the mixture is smooth.

Makes 1 cake

{index}

A
Apple and Date Loaf, 173
Apple Muffins with Spicy Topping, 170
Asparagus and Crème Fraîche Pancakes, 27
Asparagus Filo Rolls, 16
Asparagus Slice, 48
Aubergine Cannelloni, 58

B
Bacon and Tuna Tart, 28
Bacon-wrapped Lamb Chops, 118
Bahmi Goreng, 58
Baked Bean Boats, 52
Baked Bean Hash, 42
Baked Jam Roll, 162
Basic Barbecue Burgers, 104
Basic Omelette, 30
Basic Pancake, 26
Basic Spaghetti Sauce, 95
Basic Tart Pastry, 28
Big Eat Tart, 43
Black-eyed Bean Casserole, 150
Blueberry Chocolate Cake, 174
Boston Baked Beans, 37
Boysenberry Ripple Cake with Custard, 169
Braised Lamb Shanks in Merlot with Figs, 116
Butter Chicken, 79

C
Cajun Lamb Steaks with Grilled Summer Salad, 109
Cheat's Soufflé, 36
Cheese and Rice Croquettes, 68
Cheese and Walnut Potato Slice, 148
Cheese Burgers with Sweet Potato and Orange Salad, 104
Cheese Dip with Spicy Wedges, 16
Cheesy-topped Steak and Kidney Pies, 108
Chicken and Apricot Casserole, 89
Chicken and Asparagus Bake, 82
Chicken and Chilli Bean Enchiladas, 38
Chicken and Mushroom Pilaf, 69
Chicken and Spinach Cannelloni, 56
Chicken and Spinach Risotto, 64
Chicken Cacciatore, 78
Chicken in a Pot, 88
Chicken Jambalaya, 77
Chicken Laksa, 84
Chicken Pasta Salad with Sundried Tomato Dressing, 74
Chicken Rarebit, 15
Chicken with Mustard Crème Fraîche Sauce, 80
Chilli con Carne, 96
Chinese Chicken Nibbles, 19
Chocolate Berry Cheesecake, 172
Chunky Bacon and Kumara Chowder with Orange and Bacon Scones, 12
Classic Fish Cakes, 44
Coconut Fish Curry, 138
Corn and Asparagus Tart, 28
Corn Tarts and Variations, 20
Country Beef Casserole, 100
Cranberry and Chicken Pie, 82
Creamy Jam Tarts, 164
Creamy Lemon Tuna Dip, 16
Creamy Plum Tart, 163
Creamy Smoked Chicken Filo Pie, 76
Creamy Spinach Macaroni, 31
Creamy Tomato Sauce on Fettuccine, 56
Creamy Tropical Muffins, 172
Crispy Orange Roast Chicken with Gravy, 83
Crispy Sesame Chicken and Avocado on Pasta, 62
Curried Lamb with Ginger Mash, 112

E
Easy Apricot and Ginger Mousse, 160
Easy Chicken Vegetable Bake, 76
Eccles Cakes, 164

F
Farmhouse Roast Chicken with Roasted Baby Beetroot, 84
Fish Provençale, 138
French Beef and Mushroom Cottage Pie, 98
French Salad, 41
Frisco Grilled Fish, 141
Fruity Blueberry Self-saucing Pudding, 160
Fruity Devilled Sausages, 97

G
Glazed Meatloaf, 94
Golden Plum Pork Loin Chops, 131
Green Thai Vegetable Curry, 149
Grilled Focaccia with Tomato Salsa, 16
Grilled Summer Salad, 50

H
Ham and Courgette Pasta, 130
Hearty Beef and Beer Casserole, 98
Herbed Porcupines, 103
Honey Chicken with Avocado and Orange Salad, 74
Hot Potato and Bacon Salad, 51
Hummus, 14
Hunter-style Chicken on Rice, 85

I
Indian Potato and Tomato Curry, 154

K
Kedgeree, 24

L
Lamb Kebabs, 110
Lamb Korma Curry, 113
Lamb Noodle Stir-fry, 114

Lamb Pitas with Tomato Yoghurt Chilli Sauce, 121
Lamb Provençale, 111
Louise Cake, 170

M
Made-in-one-pan Dinner, 36
Maiden Tarts, 164
Meatballs in Madras Curry, 94
Mediterranean Meatballs on Pasta, 126
Mexican Beef and Bean Casserole, 102
Mexican Marinated Pork Loin Chops, 126
Mexican Potato Salad, 40
Mini Cheese Muffins, 18
Minted Kofta Kebabs, 119
Minted Pea Soup with Warm Blue Cheese Toasts, 14
Moroccan Chicken and Apricot Stew, 88
Mushroom and Ham Pancakes, 26
Mushroom Risotto, 70

N
No-fuss Apple Tart, 158
Noodle Crab Cakes, 42
Nutty Banoffie Pie, 168

O
One-pan Bolognaise, 106
Orange and Bacon Scones, 12
Orange and Mango Cheesecake Ice Cream, 158
Oriental Christmas Ham with Plum Salsa, 128

P
Paella, 65
Parmesan Crumbed Fish with Pesto Sauce, 144
Parsnip Bake, 152
Pasta Pie, 66
Pasta with Feta Crumble, 68
Peach and Cream Cheese Slice, 159
Peach and Roast Turkey Salad, 86
Peach Cake, 162
Peanut Slice, 170
Pork with Courgettes, 127

Potato and Parmesan Cakes with Tuscan Sauce, 153
Potato Kebabs with Avocado Dip, 18
Pumpkin and Sweet Basil Pasta, 60

Q
Quick and Easy Nachos, 44
Quick Lemon and Tuna Risotto, 64
Quick Lemon Tuna Soufflé, 32
Quick Mussel Chowder, 12
Quick Winter Roast Lamb, 122

R
Roast Beef with Mushroom Sauce, 107
Roast Cranberry Turkey, 90
Roast Pumpkin, Cashew Nut Burgers, 151
Roasted Tomato and Bean Salad, 47
Rogan Josh, 112
Rolled Roast Belly Pork with Peach Stuffing, 134

S
Satay Lamb with Crispy Noodles, 114
Sausage Hot Pot, 130
Savoury Mince Roll-ups, 120
Shepherd's Pie, 110
Smoked Chicken and Melon Salad, 86
Smoked Fish and Pasta Salad, 60
Smoked Fish and Potato Bake, 139
Smoked Fish Chowder, 12
Smoked Honey Chicken Salad, 40
Sour Cream Apple Pie, 160
Spanish Pasta Salad, 66
Spicy Lamb and Potato Pasties, 120
Spicy Plum Pork Spareribs, 132
Spicy Pork and Bean Tagine, 132
Spinach and Feta Filo Pie, 150
Strawberry Meringues, 166
Sweet Apple and Pork Braise, 132
Sweet Chilli Corn Fritters, 46

Sweet Indian Curried Eggs, 24
Sweetcorn and Ricotta Cheese Sauce, 59

T
Tandoori Tofu Kebabs with Kashmir Rice, 152
Thai Beef Salad with Chilli Lime Dressing, 106
Thai Curried Eggs on Noodles, 24
Thai-flavoured Noodle Cakes, 30
Thai-scented Burgers, 104
Thai Tuna Fritters, 66
Thai Tuna Toss, 142
Tomato and Olive Pasta, 60
Tomato Bean Hot Pot, 52
Tomato, Basil and Mozzarella Pizza, 148
Tortellini or Ravioli with Spinach Cream, 57
Tropical Baked Kumara, 46
Tropical Rice Salad, 50
Tuna and Apple Wraps, 140
Tuna Pasta Bake, 140
Tuna Sushi Salad, 142
Turkey Plum Stir-fry, 75
Turkish Lamb Casserole, 115
Tuscan Chicken, 78

V
Vegetarian Nachos, 44

W
Warm Chicken, Grape and Herb Salad, 86
Warm Tuna and Noodle Salad, 142
Winter Beef Casserole, 98
Winter Sausage Pie, 96